NIMBLE

OFF SCRIPT BUT STILL ON TRACK

NIMBLE

OFF SCRIPT BUT STILL ON TRACK

A COACHING GUIDE
FOR RESPONSIVE FACILITATION

Rebecca Sutherns, PhD

Cover Design by Oliver Sutherns
Typesetting by Eggplant Communications
Internal Design by Oliver Sutherns and Eggplant Communications
Author Photo by Hilary Gauld-Camilleri

First published 2019 by Rebecca Sutherns and Hambone Publishing

For information, contact:
Rebecca Sutherns
rebecca@rebeccasutherns.com

www.rebeccasutherns.com

ISBN 978-1-9995761-0-3

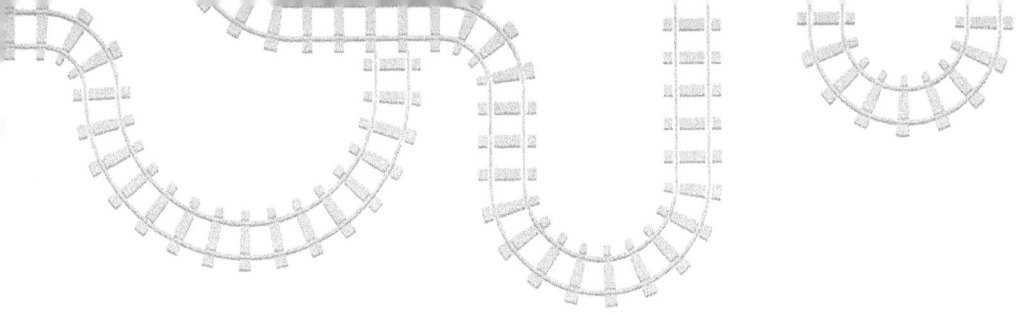

Endorsements

"Whether you are a professional facilitator or a manager who needs to run effective meetings, Rebecca has provided you with a handbook for success. Meetings don't have to be a boring, ineffective waste. They can be purposeful and, dare I say it, enjoyable. This book has the tools, process and tips to help anyone facilitate effective conversations."

– Donna McGeorge, Workplace productivity expert and author of
The 25-Minute Meeting and *The First 2 Hours*

"On track and fresh. I read it cover to cover…This should be a must-read for anyone new or struggling with facilitation. I will definitely recommend it to my colleagues."

– Rick Willis, Executive Vice President, Leadership. Eagle's Flight

"If you have ever worried about how to respond to difficulties in leading a group, you are in good company. *Nimble* is packed with valuable and practical tips for before, during and after a session, all richly illustrated from Rebecca's extensive professional experience. Your most powerful tool as facilitator is yourself – learn the Anticipation, Agility and Absorption that will give you the capacity and courage to facilitate Nimbly!"

– Martin Gilbraith, London UK - IAF Certified Professional Facilitator (CPF), Hall of Fame & past Chair; ICA Certified ToP Facilitator & ICA International past President

"In this book Rebecca thoroughly addresses critical facilitator competencies that are rarely directly taught: in particular, the IAF competencies of "Creating and Sustaining a Participatory Environment" and of practicing self-assessment and self-awareness and facilitating group self-awareness. A very useful companion to facilitation tools courses."

– Jo Nelson, CPF (IAF Certified Professional Facilitator), CTF (ICA Certified ToP Facilitator); Principal of ICA Associates, Inc.

"Make sure *Nimble* is in your arsenal of professional resources! With over 20 years of experience, Rebecca's generosity and experience shine through in this must-have facilitation playbook. A rare combination of being both concise and thorough, *Nimble* reveals the tricks of the trade for gaining mental agility and poise under pressure while keeping professionalism and humour intact. Like the 'Yes, and...' principle of improvisational theatre, Rebecca shows us that the ability to adapt and react turns out to be real time co-creation and collaboration. No wonder Rebecca Sutherns is a leader in her field."

– Nancy Watt. Improviser, Writer, Facilitator. President of NANCY WATT COMMUNICATIONS, Conservatory Graduate, Second City Toronto

"*Nimble* gives you practical guidance and insights on the mindset, preparation, behaviour and practice of facilitation and how to adapt and respond. A nice 'slice' into the market of facilitation and full of great insights and tips. There's no other way than to be... nimble!"

– Lynne Cazaly. Speaker, Facilitator and Author of 6 books including *Leader as Facilitator, ish: The Problem with our Pursuit for Perfection and the Life-Changing Practice of Good Enough, Visual Mojo* and *Making Sense.*

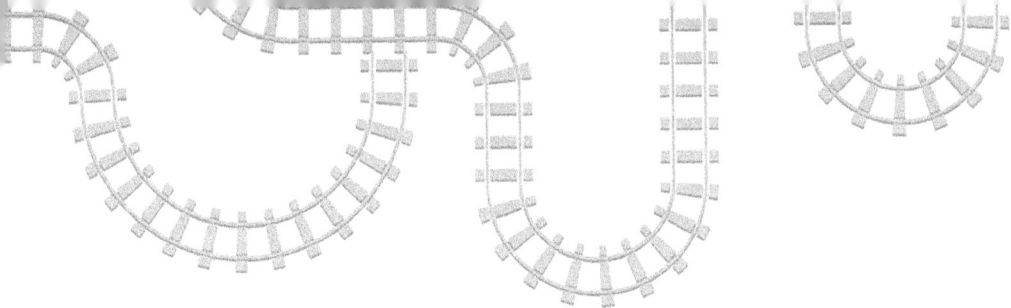

Acknowledgements

Writing is a solitary activity, but a book is never written alone. This one was written over many years in boardrooms, conference centres, community spaces and offices around the world, as I learned facilitation by doing it. I'm grateful to the countless clients and collaborators who let me learn with them—especially those who provided fodder for my ability to speak from experience about things going off the rails!

I am grateful for the friends, family members and colleagues who believed I could do this before I did and who were fans of the book even before it came out, because they've been unwavering fans of mine. I am especially appreciative to have stumbled upon Col Fink and the rest of the team at Thought Leaders Business School, who have given me a structure, role models and a whole lot of encouragement to get this done.

There's been a team of technical experts behind the scenes getting this book out of my head, off my desk and into your hands. Special thanks go to Laurie Watson, Michelle Phillips, Susan Fish, Sonia Preisler and Oliver Sutherns for that. Thanks too to the reviewers whose feedback made the book better.

And most importantly, there's been my crew at home. I do this work with and for them, because it's always been about the whole picture. Their support has been steadfast, practical and essential. Much love to Tim, Jonah, Genevieve, Claire and Hannah, and the Grandmas for that and so much more.

Rebecca Sutherns

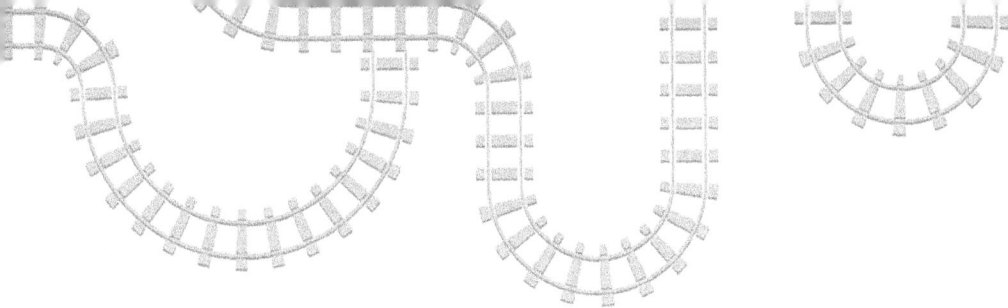

Contents

Introduction

"Everyone has a plan 'til they get punched in the mouth."

I never thought I'd start my first book with a quote from a boxer. But Mike Tyson's famous words are particularly apt when it comes to facilitation and the unpredictability of group interactions. If you've ever planned a meeting that's gone way differently than anticipated, this book is for you. If you've ever wished you'd handled an unexpected challenge better, or wanted to do a whole meeting over again, this book is for you. When you are up in front of a group, you need to be nimble—agile enough to dodge that punch—because real life will rarely match the script in your head. Sometimes it happens in very uncomfortable ways. Let me help you avoid that punch in the mouth.

We have all spent too long in unproductive meetings, with a sense of the group spinning its wheels. Life's too short. Badly run meetings, workshops, conference sessions, or even conversations, are a sign of disrespect. Your time is valuable, and I am confident that you are not interested in wasting others' time either. Allow me to equip you to invest your time well and to help others do the same.

If you're a group process facilitator, this book is for you. You plan and run meetings all the time. You have skills, experience, and a fairly deep toolbox of facilitation techniques on which you rely. You are generally comfortable at the front of the room, or you're becoming that way. But maybe, like me, you have found that traditional facilitation training focuses too heavily on how to run specific group activities. You might have been taught how to pull those activities together into a coherent design. But you haven't got strategies to help you when things don't unfold according to your carefully crafted script, *which is almost inevitably the case.*

Facing the unexpected is the norm—a reflection of the fact that we are dealing with humans, not robots—and it's what makes this job exciting.

Let this book be your coaching guide, an encouraging voice in your head, keeping you calm and focused as you navigate those unforeseen moments. When you've reached the limits of your tools, this book can extend your skills into those potentially awkward spaces in between. It can equip you to pivot with grace onto a new path without the group even noticing. It can infuse you with confidence when you would otherwise feel on the verge of becoming unnerved.

Maybe you don't think of yourself as a facilitator at all, but you do spend too much of your life in meetings. Often this is as a manager or team leader. Same people, same meeting room, same agenda, month after month. This book is for you. Not only can it help you deal with chronic frustrations and unexpected curve balls thrown at you by your team, but it can also provide you with the tools and the confidence to launch a few intentional curveballs of your own. Not simply for the sake of shaking things up, but in order to unleash greater engagement and creativity. Sometimes we need to be nimble because the unexpected happens, but other times we *need* a bit more of the unexpected to happen in order to shift the dynamic and hold more purposeful, productive conversations. Familiar teams can be like a family in which we think we know what people are likely to say, and therefore we stop listening well. This coaching guide can help you keep people closer to the edges of their seats. It's a position from which more exciting things happen.

If you chair meetings, perhaps on a board of directors or as a volunteer chair of a committee, this book is for you. It will equip you with skills to move beyond walking the group through a sterile agenda to facilitating engaging group processes that bring out the very best in your team. Being passionately committed to a cause is not enough to channel people's energies productively. In fact, passion alone can be exhausting and inefficient for those you're trying to motivate. They need a structured process to guide their collaboration, but also one that is flexible enough to adapt to the rapid pace of change. Let this book help you design and navigate your leadership road map, including knowing when to take productive detours and how to avoid potholes along the way.

If you are a trainer or a teacher, with lesson plans to follow and curriculum to deliver, this book is for you. For some of you, your lesson plans rarely match what happens in the room. When you are working from a tight script, that variability is a source of frustration or panic. For others, your lessons always match your script exactly. That too is a problem, as it's likely that you are being driven too strongly by your content rather than responding to the specific needs of your learners. This book can help you balance your solid preparation with an ability to flex with the emerging priorities of your learners. The result will be a more relevant and satisfying learning experience for all involved, and one that matches the evolving dynamic of the room.

Or perhaps you are a negotiator, whether a professional or an unpaid one (otherwise known as a parent)! This book is for you. You frequently find yourself in high-stakes conversations where intense emotions are the norm, including your own. When we care deeply about a particular outcome, it's easy to become entrenched in our position or preferred approach. This is a bit like letting our knees lock on the tennis court instead of staying loose and ready to change direction on short notice. Even when we don't have a direct stake in the result, we can become locked down when trying to negotiate between two parties that are pushing for different outcomes. It takes a lot of agility to keep on top of a conversation where new information or heated feelings are getting thrown around. When the dynamics of the conversation in front of you are all you can see, this book will offer you practical tips to help you keep the long view in mind

Whatever your context, if you've experienced that panicky feeling of leading a session when things go off script, (or wished you had a script in the first place), you've come to the right place. Even if you've avoided that experience up to now, I'm confident that you don't relish the thought of it. Preventing that off script panic is one part of the puzzle. Reaching your own potential is the other. Maybe the fear of things going off script has kept you from stepping up to the front of the room in the first place, and you've missed opportunities as a result. Allow me to ease your fears. This coaching guide will provide you with practical strategies to employ before, during and after your sessions. These are strategies that will allow you to leave feeling satisfied with both the progress your people made and the experience you shared doing so. It will help you keep a meeting moving forward productively and to bring it back on track quickly when it threatens to go off the rails. It will equip you with the tools to prepare well, then give you the confidence to hold your carefully crafted plan surprisingly loosely. It is at this point of balance that you will reach mastery in your craft.

I can assure you that this book is based on deep experience.

I have worked for more than 20 years as a professional facilitator. I have served hundreds of clients—across public, not-for-profit and private sectors and in multiple countries—in my role as founder and CEO of Sage Solutions (sage-solutions.org and rebeccasutherns.com), a strategic facilitation consulting company based in Canada. I am regularly asked to consult by Executive Directors, boards of directors, elected and appointed government leaders, collaboratives working across agencies and sectors, leadership teams and individual leaders. They rely on me to support them in issues of strategic importance, through planning, stakeholder engagement and effective governance. More than 95% of my business comes from repeat clients or referrals directly from those clients, who report counting on me to drive results while maintaining flexibility to adapt plans and processes in response to their changing needs. I also teach postgraduate courses in Facilitation Skills, Community Engagement and Not-for-Profit Governance, and online facilitation agility courses to learners around the globe. I have sat on numerous boards and community committees as a volunteer. I have organized successful events. I am a trained mediator and have applied those skills in my paid and unpaid work—including as a parent of four. The practical strategies in this book are thus grounded in that varied experience.

I am confident in the relevance of this book because it draws on my daily familiarity with needing to plan well, then adapt. I'll share many stories of having done so, both well and not so well. One of the most valuable skills

I bring to my clients is the ability to be nimble—to adjust to their varied circumstances. I am convinced that nimbleness is a teachable skill that can be learned preventatively, rather than only after you've experienced that sinking feeling in the pit of your stomach at the front of the room! We all wish for the benefit of hindsight. Let me lend some of my 20/20 hindsight to you in advance.

Some years ago, my husband and I decided to take a sabbatical, so we set off for New Zealand with our four children. One of the planned highlights for one of my daughters was skydiving. In Canada, when you're 14 years old, you can't skydive. But in New Zealand, apparently you can. She raised all the money herself ahead of time, several hundred dollars to fund her jump and photos and video footage of the experience. Let me tell you, this was not a parenting highlight for me! Sure, the fundraising responsibility piece was, but the actual experience wasn't. The night before, I had a complete meltdown about it. What mother would let her child jump out of an airplane by choice?

But the next morning, as we arrived at this beautiful skydiving spot at the northern tip of the South Island, I had a realization. My daughter was jumping tandem with an instructor who does about twenty jumps a day. It certainly was not in his interest for this to be an unsafe activity. In fact, he had a huge vested interest in it going well!

Reading Brené Brown's new book *Dare to Lead*[1] brought me back to that experience in my mind, and put another spin on it. She uses the analogy of the importance of teaching landing skills before a skydiver jumps. You don't teach those skills after they've crashed and you don't teach them during the fall. And similarly, she says, you don't teach resilience after a person needs resilience. You teach it in advance as best you can.

That, in a nutshell, is the intention of this book. *Nimble* is about preventative maintenance. It's teaching that landing skill before you jump. After all, facilitation can feel like jumping out of a plane at times! You know you're going to land, even if you're not sure the exact route you're going to take to get there, and you need some reassurance that you will know what to do when that critical moment comes. I would much rather have had Genevieve learn how to land in advance rather than being expected to figure it out after the fact or in the midst of her free fall. So to avoid that pit of your stomach awful feeling of "I have no idea how to land this thing", this book is a way that you can learn facilitation landing skills in advance, and then jump with confidence.

A note about how I'm using vocabulary so you don't get stuck:

- "Facilitation" is when someone provides a structure for people to make better decisions together. It is a process in which groups are guided to reach decisions, generate new ideas, or resolve conflicts. It occurs even if you don't think of yourself as a facilitator. Anyone who has led a conversation or run a meeting has acted as a facilitator in some capacity.

- In a professional sense, a "facilitator" is different from a trainer or a consultant or teacher—each can have their own professional associations and titles on their business cards. But here, I use the term facilitator to mean "leader of group process" who brings a suite of skills and sensibilities to a variety of roles. A facilitator does not preach, teach or share advice, but rather creates an environment where the audience discovers information or becomes aware of behaviours they may not see without help. I will use a mix of male and female pronouns to acknowledge that a facilitator can be anyone.

- "Nimble" refers to being quick and light in action or comprehension. It conveys a sense of adjusting well and on the fly, in response to whatever circumstances face you.

- "Agility" is used here in its grounded, colloquial, dictionary definition sense of adaptability and nimbleness. It is not used in reference to its more technical use in software and project management circles when associated with Lean design principles, although admittedly they share some similarities at times.

- "Script" refers to your facilitation plan. This can be either in its documented form or in its implicit form in your head. There are large variations in the style of script that people use. They can be formal or informal, detailed or loose. It's how you plan for things to go.

- "In the room" can refer to an in-person or a virtual space. I use the term to refer to anytime you're in the action of facilitating a group process. It is the live facilitation time in front of the group you're working with.

- "Sponsor" and "client" both denote the person to whom you are accountable for the outcomes of the session you are facilitating. If you are brought in as an external expert, that person is your client. If you are facilitating an internal group, you may be working with a colleague who is sponsoring the gathering. In some contexts, such as volunteer community groups, there may not be a clear sponsor. In this case, you may be informally accountable to your peers instead.

WHY IS BEING NIMBLE IMPORTANT?

Too often, facilitation skills training is about techniques and tools. Occasionally, it addresses process design. But in my experience, a well-stocked toolbox and a beautiful facilitation plan only take you about 60-70% of the way toward a successful meeting. In real life, your agility and flexibility, and your willingness to hold your script loosely, will take you the rest of the way.

Why does it matter if you are unable or unwilling to flex with what actually happens in the room? It matters for two main reasons. First, instead of facilitation saving the group valuable time, you risk having your contribution *cost* the group time, by allowing it to collectively lose its way and/or fail to achieve the purpose of the gathering. Collaborative efforts are expensive. Do the math.

Your facilitated session needs to accomplish more than the value each individual could have generated by working for the same amount of time.

The bar is set high, so if your facilitation plan does not respond to the needs in the room, the stakes are also high.

Second, you sacrifice credibility by becoming the Oblivious Facilitator. We will meet this person several times along the way. She is the one who loses the trust of the group by appearing tone-deaf to what people are communicating. She continues stubbornly along the path she earlier decided was best, without taking into account the group dynamics or new inputs brought into the process. She thereby makes the meeting about her rather than about its purpose or the group itself. Instead of masterful facilitation happening invisibly and almost magically, it becomes too obvious in its absence, and therefore is an unhelpful distraction.

OFF SCRIPT VS. OFF TRACK

In meetings with human beings, things going off script is not the exception; it's the rule. Further, my assertion is that going off script may not be a problem—in fact, it is often exactly what needs to happen in the room. The script rests with the facilitator, not the group. It should be malleable. Adapting it is not necessarily an indication of inadequate preparation or subpar facilitation skills. In fact, it may be indicative of stellar performance, as it demonstrates that you are aligned with the group and their needs. In short, you are avoiding my largest facilitation pet peeve: being oblivious or tone deaf to what's happening in the room. If you are modifying your plan, presumably you are doing so in response to the ideas of the other people sharing your space. That's exactly as it should be. Deviating from your script in response to the needs of the group and in service to the purpose of the gathering is a sign of skillful, nimble facilitation. The group might need to take a different route than the one you planned to get to their intended destination. But they are still getting there.

In contrast, going off track carries a more negative connotation. I also refer to this as going off the rails. When this happens, not only is the group process deviating from your plan, but it is straying from accomplishing its intended purpose. Chris Anderson in his book *TED Talks* refers to this as the "throughline;" the connecting theme that ties together the narrative element in a play, a movie, a novel, a talk or in this case a workshop.[2] Losing sight of the throughline can happen in various ways. You'll notice it when the group's progress toward its purpose has stalled. Facilitated processes should lead to time being well spent and more getting done. Struggling to reach a goal is to be expected, but a prolonged sense of a group spinning its wheels without any forward movement is problematic. There is an experiential difference between feeling challenged and feeling truly stuck—especially if that stuckness comes as a result of an unproductive, poorly designed process. A group should not feel stuck for long if things are truly on track.

Another example of a facilitated session going off track happens when the process is not leading to wiser decision-making. At their best, collaborative processes should harness multiple perspectives that result in more insightful conclusions than any one individual could make alone. If lowest common denominator decisions or groupthink is winning the day, the session may be off the rails.

Yet another way a meeting could go off track occurs when the implicit or explicit commitments group members have made to one another are not being honoured. If disrespectful behaviour is occurring, or even if the session is simply running overtime, those are indications that facilitation agility is required.

It takes discernment to know the difference, in the moment, between being off script and off track. Assessing the productivity of a group's pause, detour, or conflict is part of the "special sauce" of skilled facilitation. In the midst of the messiness of human interaction, it is common for some participants to judge a meeting as being well on track while others would say the opposite. This is where a facilitator must have earned the trust of the group, acting as (and being perceived as) a reliable guide who will see the group through to greater clarity.

I am working from the general assumption that it is more desirable for a meeting to stay on track than to go off it. But what about situations where the group is no longer making progress toward its intended destination *because the destination itself needs to change*? In that case, going off the rails is a positive, even necessary experience. Sometimes a group will go in an unexpected direction that uncovers a new purpose that is far better or more necessary right now than the one originally set. This too is a judgment call. If the revised track is preferable, then confirm that with the group and carry on. Once you have done so, staying on that new track is once again preferable to deviating from it.

Both experiences of a meeting going off script and off the rails require a facilitator to be nimble and quick to adapt, and to apply the coaching tips outlined in this book. I will help you become more comfortable with being off script so that going off track happens far less often. And when it does, you can recognize it sooner and course-correct before the session goes fully off the rails.

SCAFFOLDING THAT STRUCTURES THIS BOOK

Recognizing that a session is heading off the rails is a different skill than diagnosing how or why it got there, and different again from steering it back on course. There are discernible patterns to why group sessions go off the rails. The cause might be related to the people, the purpose, the place, or the process. Effective treatment of the problem is usually dependent on accurate diagnosis. If you're in trouble during a facilitation session, quickly ask yourself which of these four interrelated Ps might be responsible for what is happening in the room—it will help you head to the most helpful set of solutions in a hurry. These four Ps act as scaffolding for the structure of this book.

People. Reasons for going off the rails can include a lack of trust in the facilitator, based on her/his identity and/or behaviours; problematic relational dynamics among the participants that often pre-date the meeting; or individual or small group behaviours that hijack or distract from effective group process in the meeting.

Purpose. Reasons in this category are related to a lack of clarity or transparency about the purpose(s) of a session, a lack of relevance of that purpose, and/or a loss of focus on it. Further problems can be caused over spoken or unspoken disagreement over what purpose the group is working towards.

Place. This category of reasons is about context. Features of the meeting venue itself can negatively impact a session or the group's feelings about it. Similarly, the "vibe" in the room or the environment in which a conversation takes place has a direct effect on a meeting's productivity.

Process. This category focuses on times when the group's sequence of structured activities or outputs are not contributing meaningfully to the achievement of its purpose, resulting in a sense of being lost or stuck. This can be because the activities aren't connected well enough to the outcome, or because a theoretically useful activity is being dragged out and used ineffectively.

The other key element of structure for this book is chronology, based on phases of facilitation—that is, what needs to happen in advance of the meeting, during the session, or afterwards. Again, this allows you to flip directly to the part of the book relevant to the area you're working on at the moment. In advance, the key skill you need is anticipation. In the room, you need agility. Afterwards, what is required is absorption. We will therefore explore the four Ps within each of those timeframes and skills as follows:

	In advance ANTICIPATION	In the room AGILITY	Afterwards ABSORPTION
PEOPLE	About you About others	About you About others	About you About others
PURPOSE	Clarify it Use it	Clarify it Use it	Clarify it Use it
PLACE	Leverage it Learn from it	Leverage it Learn from it	Leverage it Learn from it
PROCESS	Script it Hold it loosely	Script it Hold it loosely	Script it Hold it loosely

Within each of the intersections above, we will explore two areas where nimble facilitation is both required and achieved. Within the category of People, we will turn the lens first toward ourselves and then toward others. Within Purpose, we will affirm the need first to clarify it and then to use it. With Place, we will first leverage it and then learn from it. Finally, within Process, we will learn first to script it and then to hold it loosely—resulting in a structure that looks like this:

	In advance ANTICIPATION	In the room AGILITY	Afterwards ABSORPTION
PEOPLE	About you About others	About you About others	About you About others
PURPOSE	Clarify it Use it	Clarify it Use it	Clarify it Use it
PLACE	Leverage it Learn from it	Leverage it Learn from it	Leverage it Learn from it
PROCESS	Script it Hold it loosely	Script it Hold it loosely	Script it Hold it loosely

Throughout the book I'll use stories to highlight key lessons learned along the way, as well as referencing other good resources in particular areas.

NIMBLE IS ALMOST INVISIBLE

Masterful facilitation is actually invisible. Done well, people hardly notice facilitation—they're just carried along, willingly and productively. They have found that sweet spot, where orchestration and improvisation offset each other beautifully.

The Balance of Nimble Facilitation

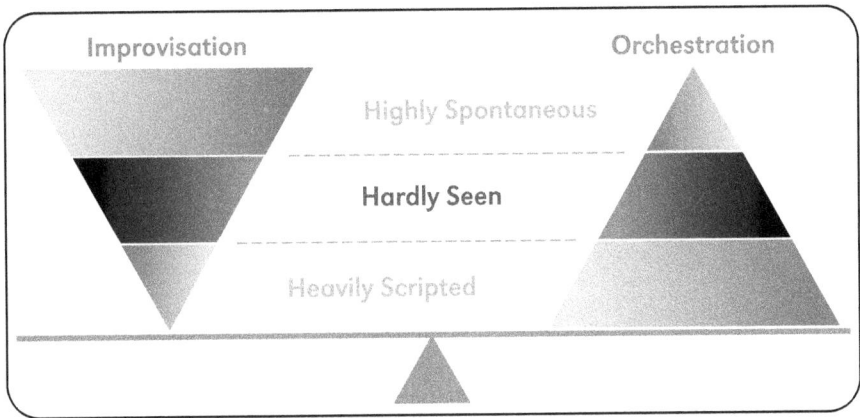

Yet most of us tend to err on one side or the other, either over-scripting or under-preparing. In the first case, we hold too tightly to our highly orchestrated script and fail to respond helpfully to shifting dynamics in the room. In the second, we bring too much of a "wait and see what happens" approach into the space, preferring to act spontaneously and improvise rather than prepare.

Before we dive into the details of learning how to find that middle ground—where your need for agility is lower and your readiness to be nimble is higher, and where you are prepared to move nimbly back and forth to more/less scripting as needed—it will be helpful for you to discern where your natural or current default position is.

If you are someone who feels more relaxed with a highly detailed agenda in your hand, or verbatim speaking notes on the podium in front of you,

you are likely in the "heavily scripted" camp. While this can be an asset, sometimes you are probably like the tennis player with locked knees and flat feet who misses the shot because he moved into position just a moment too late. In facilitation, your challenge is to loosen your grip on your notes and learn to breathe just as deeply as you did while you were feverishly clutching them.

On the other hand, if your style usually involves charming a crowd and winging it, I hope to convince you of the value of more thorough preparation as you move toward the middle from the territory of the highly spontaneous. If you were on the tennis court, you might find yourself flailing, having not perfected the technique of your strokes. In a facilitated session, your challenge is to develop discipline and rigour that will provide scaffolding within which your creativity can flourish.

The series of eight questions on the next page can help you gain self-awareness for where you sit on the spectrum of improvisation and orchestration. Place an X on the line in the place that feels most right to you. Once you've answered all eight questions, imagine that the lines are like a teeter totter. Run your eyes down the middle of the page and you'll get a good sense of where the balance tips.

As you navigate this book and your facilitation journey, take note of where you currently comfortably sit. You may be surprised at how that position shifts over time, to that magical, invisible and highly effective place of nimble facilitation.

Self-awareness Quiz

1. Doing something on short notice:

   terrifies you   ◄ – – – – – – – – – – – – ►   excites you

2. Your meeting agendas contain:

   lots of detail   ◄ – – – – – – – – – – – – ►   a basic outline

3. When you give a talk you:

   write it verbatim   ◄ – – – – – – – – – – – – ►   put key points on your slides

4. When you plan an event, you:

   triple check all the details   ◄ – – – – – – – – – – – – ►   assume all will be well

5. With a speech, you're more likely to:

   rehearse it   ◄ – – – – – – – – – – – – ►   let it flow from a rough outline

6. If someone provides you with a detailed agenda but doesn't follow it, you:

   get stressed   ◄ – – – – – – – – – – – – ►   barely notice

7. When you go on vacation, you:

   plan each day's activities   ◄ – – – – – – – – – – – – ►   let things unfold

8. Your plan for next weekend is:

   already in place   ◄ – – – – – – – – – – – – ►   What!? That's still five days away!

In advance: Anticipation

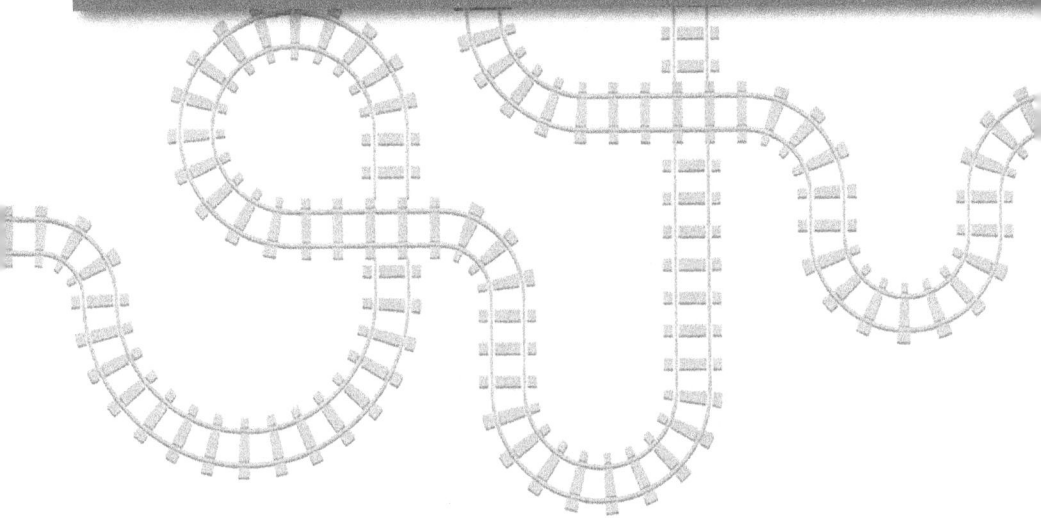

Why Plan?

This section is grounded on two core assumptions:

1. Meetings should be designed; and

2. Preparation is prevention.

Circulating an agenda is not the same as designing a meeting.

An agenda alone is not enough. Think of it as a necessary but insufficient condition on the road to productive group decision making. It's like saying you want to go on a trip, and highlighting a few of the signs along the way, without identifying specifically where you are going or how you intend to get there. We have all attended meetings that had a well laid-out agenda but were terrible. What they lacked was process design. We need to consider not only *what* topics will be covered, but also *how* they will be addressed in the room.

Even brief, run-of-the-mill meetings require deliberate design. It could be argued that it's the repetitive meetings that benefit from creative design most of all, to avoid falling into a rut of familiarity. If you can't come up with a purpose for the gathering, and a series of engaging conversations to have within it to achieve that purpose, don't have the meeting at all. Common sense perhaps, but we've all worked in situations where weekly update meetings or monthly team meetings happen because they have been scheduled, rather than because there is a compelling need for them to occur. "Because it's Wednesday" is not a good enough reason to hold a meeting.

Effective meetings happen courtesy of intentional and thoughtful preparation. The reverse is also true: when things go badly in a session, very often the causes can be traced back to a failure to prepare well. Consider the parallels with an athlete running a big race. This chapter is equivalent to the runner's nutrition and training. He doesn't just show up at the starting blocks; he has spent countless hours at the gym and on the track. Preparation is critically important, and it takes far longer than the race itself. As the poster at my daughters' dance studio says: "You earn your trophies at the studio. You just pick them up at competition."

You might say, "But, isn't this a book about being nimble and adjusting on the fly? I don't need to read about meeting planning—I was expecting exactly the opposite." Here's the connection: You don't need to adapt to the unexpected when you see it coming in the first place. Thoughtful preparation can preclude or limit the need for facilitation agility. 83% of people understand that accidents are largely preventable, even if they are not intentional.[3] No one intends for a session to go off the rails, yet most of the time they could have prevented it from doing so. So we're starting with prevention as the first and probably most important step to being an agile facilitator at the front of the room. Preparation is preventative.

Moreover, being nimble is not the same as "winging it." Just like the best improvisational jazz musicians have been equipped by their classical training, or contemporary dancers have been prepared by countless hours at the ballet barre, so too should the work of the most responsive of facilitators be underpinned by detailed planning and solid technique. It is actually easier to be productively flexible when you start with a structure from which to deviate. As Donna McGeorge says, "The best and most professional people are those who practice, plan and prepare for their meetings. It may look like they are winging it, but it's their preparation that makes it effortless."[4]

We know this from research on creativity. Perhaps counterintuitively, creativity flourishes when it has edges and constraints. "Without boundaries to define it, there is no creative territory."[5] Creativity tends to be unfocused and unintentional when it lacks structure or guidelines. Instead, we want to be intentional in the way we generate new ideas. We need to create the conditions for creativity to flourish.[6] These constraints are not meant to hinder but rather to invoke your creative senses to create more mindfully. David Usher explains that people often shy away from "pink elephant thinking"—big, wild ideas—dismissing them immediately because they seem impossible or not grounded in reality. However, allowing yourself to play, unbound by common sense, ushers in creativity.[7] The confluence of freedom and structure turn those ideas into tangible outcomes. Once realized, your idea will likely be much smaller, so start big.

A third reason for committing to thorough preparation is that we must be willing to embrace complexity in order to address it well.[8] This does not mean adhering to a strict cause and effect expectation that a session will unfold along a linear path. Rather, it means having clarity about what must happen so that you can allow for lots of diversity to surface around the other stuff.[9] Creating a strong but flexible structure is one way to apply that learning to a facilitated context; you need to prepare well to clarify the destination and perhaps a couple of key milestones along the way, while anticipating that the routes to get there will take unexpected twists.

A final reason for embracing the need to plan thoroughly comes from the field of motivation: neither success nor failure is ever an accident.[10] Planning allows you to set your intention clearly and firmly on a successful outcome. Figure out what you want, find out how much that costs, and resolve to pay the price. If what you want is an engaging, productive collaborative experience, the price is disciplined preparation.

In facilitation, the key to effective preparation is anticipation. Accurate foresight is protective against unexpected pitfalls. In other words, if you know what is about to happen, you can plan for it. In this chapter, we'll explore how to strengthen your ability to anticipate accurately how participants are likely to respond in a room.

Yet even when we predict correctly, we are not always thoroughly prepared. (I know I'll need to eat three times per day—why is my refrigerator empty?) We need hacks and disciplines to translate that knowledge into reliable, habitual behaviours that will serve us well from the front of the room.

And even with the best of preparation, we know that deviations from the script will inevitably happen. Although the specific timing of accidents cannot be predicted, their overall periodic occurrence can be. Planes crash. Ships sink. Accidents are a "normal" part of the risk of operating a complex system[11]—and multi-stakeholder collaboration is definitely complex. At those times, solid preparation is still our friend, as it can also help us cope more effectively with the things we failed to see coming.

Usually accidents are caused by a series of small events rather than a single catastrophic error. You can't plan for every contingency, and there are countless reasons why a session can go off the rails. This chapter will help you ensure that your poor preparation is not one of them.

People

	In advance **ANTICIPATION**	In the room **AGILITY**	Afterwards **ABSORPTION**
PEOPLE	**About you About others**	About you About others	About you About others
PURPOSE	Clarify it Use it	Clarify it Use it	Clarify it Use it
PLACE	Leverage it Learn from it	Leverage it Learn from it	Leverage it Learn from it
PROCESS	Script it Hold it loosely	Script it Hold it loosely	Script it Hold it loosely

The first category to consider in your advance preparation is people. Right from the start, your focus should be on the people who will be in the room and what they need in order for the session to be a roaring success. The first thing they need is for you to be at your best. They also need to be operating within a context of relational trust so that they too can function at their best in the room.

ABOUT YOU

Self-preparation is self-preservation

Well before you step into the room to facilitate a meeting, there are preparatory steps you can take to equip yourself to do well. This preparation builds your capacity regardless of the specific situation facing you. We will highlight two skills here: building self-awareness and building your technical proficiency.

Know yourself

The self-help section in any bookstore is rapidly expanding.[12] You may be someone who devours self-improvement books or someone who thinks pop psychology is a waste of time. Either way, you will be more likely to avoid being the Oblivious Facilitator if you have taken the time to cultivate a healthy sense of self-awareness before walking in the room.

What's the link between knowing yourself and being a nimble facilitator? As a facilitator, your main tool is yourself.[13] You are not interchangeable with anyone else. Despite lots having been written about the benefits of facilitator neutrality,[14] your specific presence does affect the dynamic. You therefore need to pay attention to what you, as a person, bring into the room. For example:

- You need to know what you require in order to be on top of your game. Do you need a lot of sleep? Get it. Do you tend to suffer an attack of nerves before starting a session? Develop a mantra and routine that will serve as a counterattack. Are you aware that a particular personality type or behaviour in the group is likely to irritate you? Have a plan for how you'll handle it if it comes up. You need to be "match ready" every time.

- Your role as the facilitator intersects with other aspects of your identity to shape how others perceive or interact with you. If you are an older white male appointed to facilitate a contentious session by the Chair of the board, that matters. If you are a young woman of colour who is brand new to this group, that matters too. Facilitators are trained to recognize power dynamics in a room—don't be oblivious to the dynamics that involve you.

- Your personal style affects your facilitation practice. People feed off (or are put off by) the energy of others. Be aware of how your energy affects how others experience your leadership. In my case, I am an enthusiastic fast talker who processes information quickly. As a result, I facilitate dynamic, engaging sessions. But I can also move through activities too quickly for some participants who would prefer that I slow the pace, explain things more thoroughly, and allow more time for them to reflect on the questions being asked. I have many choices open to me as to how to leverage and temper my energetic style—but the first step is awareness that it does affect many elements of the sessions I lead.

- Your temperament and experiential preferences will also likely affect your design. If you love to chat, you are more likely to include conversational activities in your facilitation plan. If you don't see yourself as a creative mind, you're less likely to write a plan which demands idea generation and imagination. Pay attention to which styles might be left out or overused because of your personality being inserted into your planning, and which participants' preferences might be excluded as a result.[15]

- Your tolerance for risk or ambiguity is also unique to you. A situation that makes me uncomfortable might be energizing to someone else. I might be fine with a very loose agenda, while another facilitator (or perhaps my client) might feel calmer with a highly detailed facilitation plan in hand. Therefore, even our definitions of what constitutes a session being "off the rails" will vary with who we are and how we prefer to work. No judgment is intended here. I have experienced outstanding facilitation by people embodying a variety of temperaments, including folks who are highly introverted. What matters is not the specifics of your own style, but rather, your awareness of that style.

You may even find yourself working with someone who has a very different style to your own. I have co-facilitated a session with a very skilled colleague whose tolerance and need for detail is much higher than mine. She works from a much more detailed script, and yet the very things that she finds reassuring—highly specific times and concrete words—make me hyperventilate! Feeling constrained makes me stressed. I prefer big chunks of time that indicate roughly what we're doing. As long as I'm clear how long the chunk is, and what its intended purpose is, I'm settled.

Yet equally, what gives me flexibility within a structure causes my colleague to become stressed. To work together successfully, we needed to find a compromise that would allow us each to operate in a relaxed state. Our solution was to have her create her detailed script, with my warning that I may or may not follow it exactly. However, my commitment to the schedule was to reassure her that at the end of each major section we would be on time and we would have achieved what we set out to achieve. In the end, neither of us followed our own styles exactly. But we both found a way to feel centred and prepared.

It's not unlike preparing to give birth. People who have a birth plan are basically seeking to lower uncertainty in a context that is highly uncertain. I often tell expectant moms that the best thing that they can do in terms of their birth plan is to think about where they are going to feel most relaxed. That's really the critical differentiator. What will it take for them to feel most at ease? The answer to that differs person to person. For some people, that relaxation comes from being in a highly medicalized environment within arm's reach of the latest technology, every pain medication and every intervention possible. That's how they feel most relaxed. Yet for other people, giving birth is going to feel better in their home. They want familiar surroundings, their own pillow, and their own bed. That's how they feel more relaxed. Know yourself.

Kristen Hansen, thought leader and neuroscience expert[16], talks about the difference in performance between when we're in a threat state versus when we're in a reward state. We perform better when we are not under stress. Our bodies perform better physiologically, and amazingly our mind is also sharper. We have more insights and we're better at problem solving. This is as true in facilitation as it is in a sports match or in an operating room. Figure out the level of preparation and detail that you need in order to operate at your very best and to be fully present in the moment. Don't be distracted by a preparation methodology that doesn't suit you, especially if it's just because you've seen someone else do it. Create a routine of preparation that makes your performance easy and relaxed.

In the initial preparation phase, it is all about you. But tread lightly when you carry that knowledge into the room itself. Just as marketing should be primarily about the customer rather than about the product, facilitation should be primarily about the group rather than about the facilitator. A carefully crafted facilitation design should be virtually invisible to participants, and a well-prepared facilitator should be too. Be careful not to let your search for self-awareness turn into running a session as if it's all about you. As renowned speaking mentor Matt Church says, "Don't do therapy on stage."[17]

You may find the following tool useful increasing your self-awareness as a facilitator. And if you aren't sure how to fill it in, be brave enough to ask for help from someone who knows you well.

Self Awareness

I tend to be someone who...	Therefore as a facilitator I am likely to be...	This is an asset because...	I may need to counterbalance this by...

Build your skills outside the room

The second dimension of personal preparation is to build the skills you will need once you get in the room. Nimble facilitation is definitely a skill that is honed with practice, but that practice need not only happen in public when the stakes are high. It can be intentionally pursued in safer, more controlled environments in advance.

For clarity, I will treat these skill sets (i.e. basic facilitation know-how and the ability to adjust under pressure) as if they are more distinct than they are in reality. In practice, if you can perfect both, the combination is powerful. It truly is what separates good facilitators from great ones.

Facilitation agility usually emerges after the more basic facilitation skills are in place. Beginner facilitators tend to accumulate a few techniques and apply them rather rigidly at first, often erring on the side of inflexible, highly scripted sessions. In fewer instances, they leave things too wide open. But in either case, the ability to be highly responsive tends to follow the consolidation of core skills such as leading a structured discussion or designing an agenda. There are many ways to build these foundational skills, but it takes time and intentional effort. Consider taking a course. Job-shadow an experienced practitioner. Or start with smaller, lower risk sessions, perhaps as a volunteer. Create opportunities to build your confidence and practice your newly acquired abilities where the stakes are lower.

It is useful to practice individual skills, then gradually layer them as your confidence builds. For example, watch a video of people having a conversation, and write down the highlights on a flip chart. Did you keep up? Did you miss anything? Is your writing legible and visible from the back of the room? Learning this way allows you to rewind and try again, rather than honing this skill in front of colleagues or clients. Another way to use that same video might be to practice what Alan Weiss calls "rapid reframing."[18] Listen to the conversation and see how quickly and accurately you can verbalize the highlights, along the lines of, "What I hear you saying is… and where I'd like to take this from here is…" Another option is to practice giving instructions out loud for each of the activities you have planned for an upcoming meeting. Perhaps you can ask someone else to give you feedback on how clearly the task was described. These practice hacks might seem artificial and awkward at first, but these are the skills that set outstanding facilitators apart. Imagine if you did not have them in place: the notes would be illegible, inaccurate and incomplete. The group's progress would be slowed while you paused to figure out what was going on and where to take things next. Your instructions might increase confusion rather than clarity. Framed that way, you can see why these foundational facilitation skills are critical. If you do not have them in place, it will be even more challenging for you to adapt well to changing conditions in the room.

One additional proficiency that traditional facilitation skills training tends to overlook has to do with strengthening your ability to deal with cognitive noise and overload. This is a necessary facilitation skill even when things in a meeting are staying well on track, but it is even more critical when they are not. Ever since J.R. Stroop's pioneering research in 1935, scientists have known that multitasking—or processing multiple incoming streams of information—is a challenge for the human brain. It slows us down, with overall brain activity dropping to less than two-thirds of what it would have been if we had done two tasks sequentially. Our brains process serially, not in parallel.[19] Task-switching also causes stress, which may in turn inhibit our short-term memory. We sacrifice depth for breadth. And unfortunately it gets worse with age.[20]

Physical task-switching and mental multitasking are part of a facilitator's job description. I think of it as operating on multiple channels at once. At a minimum, you are guiding the group through a process while monitoring to see how well people have understood your instructions. You are also thinking about whether the next activity you'd planned is likely to make sense after all, and deciding how to adapt it if not. At the same time, you might be writing on a flip chart while someone in the group is talking (harder than it looks), noticing that the coffee is running low, and checking the clock. In addition, you've observed that the meeting sponsor has pulled out his phone and that the woman sitting near the back is still not engaging in the conversation. You get the picture.

Can it get better with practice? Ironically the more we do it, the more susceptible we become to interference from irrelevant stimuli.[21] However, we can improve our performance when one of the tasks, which may have been difficult at first, becomes familiar enough to become automated in our brain.[22] We also seem to be better able to do it when tasks use two different input channels than when the tasks compete for the same pathway.[23] For example, a facilitator can more easily read her notes on a flip chart while listening to the next participant's contribution to the conversation than she can listen to two comments at once.

It is critical that you find ways to strengthen and cognitively automate your facilitation skills so that the mental multitasking required, even when things are going well, does not overload your brain to the point that you have no remaining capacity to adapt to the unexpected.

It is also possible to build your capacity to be responsive and nimble by practicing those skills in other realms, outside of a meeting context at all. Take stock of which elements of agility you are interested in strengthening. For instance, do you need practice adapting to unexpected circumstances? Team sports, improvisational theatre, live escape rooms and video games all require us to adapt quickly to changing conditions. Or perhaps you want to remain more calm under pressure, in which case mindfulness training through yoga or meditation would be valuable practices for you. Maybe you need to become more accustomed to being afraid, so that you can experience adrenaline as a performance enhancer rather than something to be avoided. When the body is flooded with adrenaline, the brain is engaged, focused, and often able to handle cognitive tasks more quickly.[24] Maybe the advice on the Lululemon shopping bag—"Do one thing a day that scares you"—isn't too far wrong.

Consider how you can "strengthen your agility muscles" in multiple contexts. Your aim is to become familiar with how your brain and body feel in that state, so that when you are in a facilitation situation on the verge of heading off track, you'll be better able to respond effectively.

Canadian astronaut Commander Chris Hadfield tells an incredible story that illustrates the power of this style of preparation. On a spacewalk outside of the space shuttle, he got something in his eyes. With zero gravity, when your eyes tear up, the tears don't fall. As a result, he could not clear out whatever was impeding his vision and he went blind in space. Although his extensive training had never included this exact scenario, he had role-played countless other stressful, unexpected situations prior to this mission. He recounts how the preparation in those circumstances allowed him to stay calm in this one. He had literally trained himself out of being afraid, a very useful skill in a situation in which most of us would most certainly be panicking.[25]

Commander Hadfield's harrowing, but ultimately successful, experience powerfully demonstrates that thorough preparation transforms fear into courage and competence. Even though we cannot accurately predict exactly what will happen, we can use rigorous preparation to make us ready to cope with whatever does occur.

ABOUT OTHERS

The power of relationships

Your personal preparation is important in equipping you to be agile in the room, but preparation is not just a solitary activity. The relationships you develop in advance can also accelerate your performance in the room. In this section, we will explore two aspects of the power of relationships as a tool for greater agility, or even for offsetting the need for it in the first place: investing in relational currency and knowing your people.

Invest in relational currency

Positive relationships make work easier. We all know who we tend to go to for help at the office. We also know that person we would rather avoid. It's just easier to do it ourselves. We can easily identify the ones we have lots of time for and people we are willing to cut more slack, as contrasted with folks we tend to be quicker to criticize. The same behaviour from a friend does not irritate us nearly as much as the identical behaviour from someone with whom we have a difficult history.

Relational currency is the secret sauce of facilitation agility.

My husband Tim, who owns an engineering company, keeps good track of how people take their coffee and tea. If he knows that someone loves green tea with milk, or that another client loves a double shot coffee, he brings those drinks to meetings already doctored up to their specifications. He remembers a lot of small details and has become known for that kind of personalized attention. Likewise, my children notice that when we go to the dentist, the staff have a way of continuing the conversation that we started together six months ago as if it was uninterrupted. They may ask how the kids' music lessons are going, or how our trip to Australia was, or how things are going with my business. Despite the fact that this knowledge is simply due to detailed record keeping—a system that the dentist has disciplined her staff to maintain—the care feels personalized because of their ability to translate those systems into natural interpersonal interactions.

In my own practice, I apply these lessons as much as possible. I happen to have a really good memory for names, my clients' children's names, and the activities that they undertake. If I can build rapport by inserting some details that are personalized and customized to the individual in the room, that builds trust and therefore allows me to quickly build some currency with people. If things go badly in the room, the group is more likely to extend grace to me than if I hadn't made an effort to connect with them. Investing in positive relationships with your participants will lead to them being more gracious with you if and when things do go off track in a session.

I include this strategy in the In advance section because relationship-building takes time and can begin well ahead of your workshop or meeting. If you have built a strong reputation with someone consistently over time, they are more likely to overlook your mistakes than if you stand in a chronic relational deficit with that person. Stephen M. R. Covey underscores this idea in *The Speed of Trust*.[26] Trust is built through keeping our commitments, big and small. When we have demonstrated our integrity over time, both through intentional investment in strengthening connections and through keeping our promises to our clients and colleagues, we earn their trust. Those investments yield returns later, including when we might be struggling through a hard day at the front of the room. It helps to have cultivated allies who think the best of us and who are willing to help us through the rough spots.

Yet we do not always have the opportunity as facilitators to build relationships with our participants over time in advance. Consider a scenario in which you have not yet worked with people coming to a session, but you can find out in advance who they are. In that case, do what you can to make contact and build rapport with them ahead of time. Practically speaking, this could mean sending a quick survey to registrants for an upcoming retreat to find out what they are most looking forward to, or circulating a video agenda rather than a traditional printable version. This extra effort creates an opportunity for participants to see and hear you describing your hopes for the session, thereby building rapport before you've even met. Or maybe you call each person by telephone, simply to express how glad you are that she is choosing to attend the event. Extending a personal touch is an opportunity to be creative. Chip and Dan Heath highlight this beautifully in *The Power of Moments*,[27] in which they assert that memorable moments are not random but can, in fact, be created.[28] Doing so will build your currency with participants so that they are "for you" when they walk in the room.

But even if you must head into a session with people who are brand new to you, you still have an opportunity to leverage this relational currency on short notice. Although we will address "in the room" behaviours in a later section in more detail, it is worth noting in your preparation phase that you should not underestimate the power of quickly establishing a positive connection with people between their arrival and the start of the session. Be ready for them. Greet them upon their arrival. Make eye contact and smile. Use their name.[29] Ask them questions about their interests and remember those details later. Build in a head start for yourself. If you've taken the time to impress people and initiate a relationship with them in multiple ways from the outset, they are less likely to notice or care if you make a small mistake or two later on.

Know your people

You can build on this relational currency by incorporating your prior knowledge of the group into your facilitation planning process, in large and small ways. If you know your client loves chocolate, put some on the tables. If you know the group has a great sense of humour, be sure to build some fun into your time together. If they are a no nonsense bunch, get right down to business. Perhaps they use a lot of acronyms. Don't slow them down by having to ask what they mean; include a glossary in your notes. Do they have a low tolerance for ambiguity? Set their expectations accurately with a warning, included in your script, that things in the meeting are likely to get messy before they get tidy again, much like cleaning out a closet. Are there sensitive topics that would best be avoided? Be sure to identify prospective landmines in your notes.

You can certainly gather this knowledge over time, as a result of having worked with a particular team more than once. But it requires intentionality and attention. You may have had ample opportunities to engage in reconnaissance missions, but if you fail to use your points of connection deliberately to gather this kind of information, these are lost opportunities. Ori and Rom Brafman have researched what it takes to accelerate our connection with another person, and they write about in *Click: The Magic of Instant Connections*.[30] They highlight the importance of vulnerability, proximity, resonance, similarity and environment. Having even one of these elements in common with someone else can vastly accelerate a connection. So as a masterful facilitator, pay attention to how you can find and build these points of connection.

If you are working with a group for the first time, you need to ask more and better questions in advance. It is easy for us to be consumed by the mechanics and logistics of an upcoming session, at the expense of inquiring about the personality of a group or the individuals within it. Do your homework. Check the client's website. Ask for a list of who will be in the room. Find out about corporate lingo so you don't use the wrong terms and look like a definite outsider. Imagine how impressive you will appear if, as a new facilitator to that team, you arrive having mined for customized details about them and leveraged that knowledge to tailor the facilitated session to match their preferences.

These tips may sound like common sense or simply good customer service, but they also contribute to effective facilitation agility. They act as deposits in what Stephen M. Covey referred to as the "emotional bank accounts" of your participants, predisposing them to be gracious to you.[31] You can bet that when my husband remembers how his clients take their coffee, and brings it to them already doctored up to their liking, they are in a more positive frame of mind before the meeting even starts. These deposits also offset the need for you to adapt on the fly. If you can accurately anticipate what is likely to work well for this particular team, and build it into your facilitation design, the likelihood of things going off the rails in the first place is considerably lower. An ounce of prevention…

Which brings us to the question: How do you obtain information about a group in advance? More specifically, from whom?

As an outside facilitator, you will be working with someone who acts as your bridge into the team or organization that has invited you in. Let's call that person your informant. The quality and accuracy of the information you obtain from that person will have a direct effect on your ability to anticipate accurately what to expect in the room and how best to design the session. Your informant's perspective can easily become yours.

But what happens if your informant is an outlier? Imagine a situation in which your informant's perspective is heavily skewed away from the majority view in the room. Perhaps she is not party to certain information. Often he is busy and has not thoughtfully considered your preparatory questions, or has forgotten to distribute your pre-work to the group. Maybe he has an axe to grind. It could just be that as a single individual, her point of view is simply limited, as is true for any of us. In any or all of these scenarios, it is not hard to imagine how you might need to be even more nimble than otherwise expected if your informant has caused you to be misinformed or underprepared.

Some time ago, I was getting ready for a two-day offsite with a senior management team of a local government. As part of my preparation, I checked in about how the group was feeling. My main contact person, who happened to be a senior person on that senior team, passed on that the group was very much looking forward to the session. She outlined what the objectives were, and certainly made it sound like everyone was on board with the agenda. This was an agenda that I had somewhat inherited, as I was doing the session on fairly short notice. Not unreasonably, I basically took her word for it.

Luckily for me, there happened to be a scheduled team meeting happening a week before the two-day offsite, and they invited me along to meet the group. Claiming only a brief agenda item on their existing meeting that day, I walked into the room to discover that they were openly hostile about the whole idea. They weren't clear on why they were doing the retreat. They had done a previous retreat before that hadn't gone well. They had other things on their schedules that were higher priorities. All in all, they were not interested in this two-day offsite even a little bit.

I was shocked by the vast gulf between the information I'd been given and the reality of the situation in front of me. I had fifteen minutes to convince them that both I and the session were worth investing in. I needed to adapt very quickly, as I knew how important it was that I build some credibility and currency with them in the limited time I had before the real event. It might've taken longer for them to get over some of the reservations that they were expressing, but because I came in explicitly to ask them what they wanted and needed out of that time, they felt heard.

By investing those few minutes in advance, we were able to get more or less on the same page. I was able to adjust the agenda accordingly and to save the situation in advance. When the two-day offsite came around, the group was in a better frame of mind and we were able to figure out together how to make that time valuable to them. The end result was a group that was productive and unified for the two days.

Even as an inside facilitator, working with a group of people with whom you are familiar, you still have a variation on an informant—yourself. If you rely only on your personal understanding of the group to anticipate what might happen in the room, you may be walking in with a bias that will not serve you well. You don't know what you don't know, so make the effort to find out your blind spots from other people around you.

In either of these scenarios, you risk having inaccurately anticipated and therefore poorly prepared for the session. Poor preparation requires far greater agility in the room than you otherwise would have needed. What can you do to mitigate the risk of an unhelpful informant?

I have found three strategies to be most helpful, especially when used in combination with one another:

1. Ask lots of questions

2. Strive for multiple points of contact

3. Do what you can yourself

The first protective strategy is to ask lots of questions about anything and everything that might affect the effectiveness of your session. These questions can range from the most basic of logistics to the more highly conceptual issues. Ask about the details of the venue, the personalities, the interpersonal dynamics, the level of enthusiasm likely to be present in the room, the process for determining the need for the session, the wording of the invitation, the importance of formal and informal hierarchies, the food... you get the idea. Answers to these questions paint a detailed picture of what you can expect. Hopefully, if your informant does not know the answers, she can find them for you. Your contact will also start to realize how important those details are to you, which might cause her to up her game!

You also want to ask good questions to check in with your own presumptions about the session. It is a truism in facilitation and elsewhere that the questions you ask shape the answers you get. Warren Berger explores how to ask better questions to override the instinct to trust our gut, because our gut might not always be right.[32] Our gut is subject to inherent biases, false confidence, and any number of decision-making pitfalls. His work is echoed by Amy Edmondson, who emphasizes the power of a genuine, direct, and curious question in contributing to psychological safety in a group or relationship.[33]

Second, always strive for multiple points of contact. In investments, a diverse portfolio is protective. In research, a larger sample size is more reliable. So too in preparing for a facilitated session. Find ways to gather various perspectives beyond just the one held by your main contact person. In practical terms, this might mean asking to meet with the senior leadership team ahead of the event, or sending a brief survey to participants in advance, or calling each participant to gather their perspective on the upcoming session. These approaches can build rapport, as explained earlier, but they are also protective because they give you a clearer sense of the diversity and dynamics likely to greet you in the room. You can thus prepare more effectively and avoid needing to adjust your plans in the room due to having received partial information.

Which leads to the third strategy of doing things yourself when you can. You know what you need to be well prepared and effective, so keep those things within your control whenever possible. For me, this means bringing my own supplies, projector and note takers to sessions. That way, I reduce unpredictability. Perhaps for you, it's something different. Relying less heavily on your informant to take responsibility for the success of the session lowers your risk of it going off the rails.

True preparation entails getting both a deep sense and a broad spread of knowledge about a group. It's not about just trusting one person's perspective on the group, but also finding ways to get multiple perspectives. Practice developing backup plans and systems to make sure that you triangulate the information you're getting from just one person. Lastly, strengthen this preparation by getting as much firsthand access to people as you can. Having a chance to learn who you're working with is invaluable. Imagine the impact you have when you recognize faces and greet them by name as they arrive the following week. Little touches like that are an incredibly powerful currency.

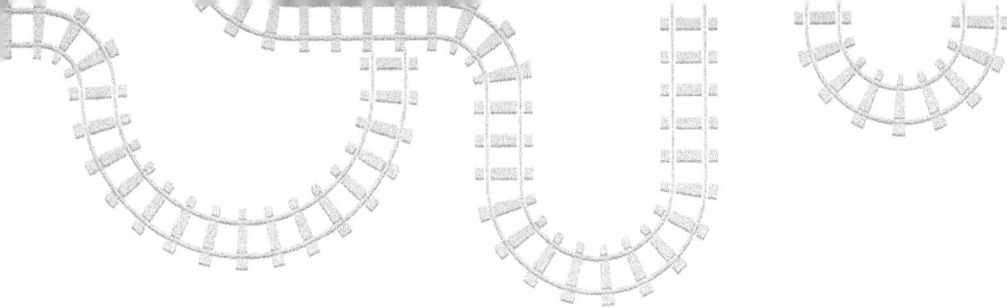

Purpose

	In advance **ANTICIPATION**	In the room **AGILITY**	Afterwards **ABSORPTION**
PEOPLE	**About you** **About others**	About you About others	About you About others
PURPOSE	**Clarify it** **Use it**	Clarify it Use it	Clarify it Use it
PLACE	Leverage it Learn from it	Leverage it Learn from it	Leverage it Learn from it
PROCESS	Script it Hold it loosely	Script it Hold it loosely	Script it Hold it loosely

The next category of preparation in advance to help you offset the need for facilitation agility in the room involves purpose—clarifying it and using it.

CLARIFY IT

A skillful facilitator is the guardian of the group's purpose. In *The Purpose Revolution*, John Izzo and Jeff Vanderwielen emphasize the centrality of purpose, highlighting its importance in guiding strategy, decision-making, allocation of resources, and most importantly relationships.[34]

The achievement of the purpose should be the facilitator's primary deliverable.

When things threaten to go off track it is therefore of paramount importance that you not lose sight of what you are trying to achieve.

In order to clarify a group's purpose, you must first insist they have one, and then design a session that aligns around it.

Insist on it

The first step toward a purpose-driven project or session involves having one. Sounds straightforward, right? You would be amazed at how many meetings have no reason for being held. "Because it's the first Tuesday of the month" is not a compelling or sufficient reason to meet. It rests with you as the facilitator to work with the sponsor to ensure the meeting does in fact have a purpose. That purpose can then act as your compass throughout the session, keeping you focused and aware of what on track actually means.

The purpose of a session is rarely self-evident, even to a meeting's organizers. Create space in your preparation plan to discuss and refine the purpose for the session. Sometimes co-creating or uncovering a meeting's true, clear purpose can take some time. It may take some insistence or coaxing on your part.

A meeting's purpose often depends on your perspective. The purpose from the vantage point of the sponsor could differ from the reasons participants have for attending, for example. Some of those purposes might be implicit or even unconscious. Yet it is critical, in the planning phase, to insist that a shared purpose, or multiple shared objectives, be explicitly communicated so that the group's work has a sense of meaning and relevance.

If, having invested time to discern and express purpose, you and the sponsor are not able to articulate why a group is gathering, you are better to cancel the session than to proceed without a shared reason for it. Purpose is that important.

Express it

Once you are confident there is in fact a reason for a meeting to be held, your job shifts to helping the sponsor articulate precisely what it is. One of the most helpful skills a facilitator can offer is the ability to succinctly capture someone's intent, using that person's words whenever possible. When the words are carefully chosen, you will want to communicate that purpose clearly and often.

Once the session's purpose is agreed upon, memorize it. Circulate it as the central feature of the agenda. Write it on the wall for all to see. Then, when things in a session get messy or unclear, that purpose statement can function as the North Star for you and the group. Use it to remind yourself of what *must* happen, and what other things you can perhaps let slide, in order to make sure you deliver on the achievement of that purpose.

Remember too that a meeting can achieve multiple objectives, or even types of objectives. As a facilitator, you are wise to help your client develop objectives related both to the content being discussed and to the experience of working on that content together. For instance, a corporate retreat might be designed to develop an annual set of priorities (content) and to build a stronger sense of unity through having fun together (experience).[35]

This concept of rational and experiential aims extends well beyond facilitated agendas. *The Trusted Advisor* authors, David Maister, Charles Green and Robert Galford, affirm that even trust itself is both rational and experiential, and a concept such as "reliability" has both objective and subjective elements—i.e. when someone shows up on time (i.e. rational/ objective) and behaves according to my personal expectations and preferences (i.e. experiential/subjective), I consider them to be reliable.[36]

While I am not a fan of the language of the rational/experiential dichotomy (as it seems to imply that experience is irrational), I do find that distinguishing between content and experience is helpful. I subdivide each category further, so that content includes both the topic to be covered (i.e. what are we talking about?) and the reason for doing so (i.e. what does "done" look like?) and experience includes both the emotional or intuitive experience of the session (i.e. was it fun?") and the methodology to be followed to get there (i.e. "what activity will we do at this point?")

Having these multiple objectives clearly articulated is not only a helpful design tool, but it also helps to gauge the success of a meeting. In a session, you may realize that you are missing the mark on the rational purpose while fully achieving the experiential aim. Consider the example of a group that gets laughing as a result of a particular activity. This jovial bunch then starts sharing other funny memories that lead to even more sustained laughter. As the facilitator, you know that this segment is now taking considerably longer than planned, to the point that the substantive objective for this section of the meeting may not be achieved on time. But you also remember that one of the experiential objectives of the workshop was to build a stronger sense of team and to enjoy time away together. So, you let the laughter run its natural course, knowing that although you may be off script in one way, you are hitting your target in other. While this example calls for nimble facilitation and clear judgment in the room, it also requires careful planning in advance to ensure that you walk into that room crystal clear about what you are trying to achieve. Keeping these big-picture priorities in mind is especially important when the objectives of a session may seem to contradict one another in the moment. (And hopefully, you can cycle back to get that substantive objective met before the end of the session!)

With multiple objectives at play simultaneously, it is therefore quite possible to be on track toward one aim while off track in terms of another. In the preparation phase, it is important to surface what those aims are and then to design the session to ensure that all of them are met.

USE IT

Once purpose has been articulated, it is time to use it to shape your facilitation planning. As John Izzo says, "What determines the effectiveness of purpose is how alive the conversation about that purpose is.[37]" Developing a discipline of articulating purpose can help you confirm who should attend the session, for example, as the purpose should be relevant to all attending. Purpose should also guide the activities chosen within a session. I will highlight two hacks to make that happen, both within a single planning tool— the Facilitation Planning Template. This template is just one of the useful frameworks provided for your benefit. As you progress through the book, other templates and documents will be shown. Should you wish to access or print other copies of these templates, please refer to the online toolkit.[38]

Address both content and process

Clear rational and experiential aims can translate seamlessly into the content and the process within your facilitation plan. It is purpose that allows you to align your methodology with the topic at hand. For example, if the content of a session revolves around "buying a new car," you have a number of different activities that could be suitable. You could choose to brainstorm ideas of possible makes, or collaboratively develop criteria for selecting the vehicle, or vote to choose between four options... each of these is a reasonable activity related to buying a new car, but without a clear purpose for the conversation (i.e. are we generating ideas or choosing between them or both), you will not know which tool to pull out of your toolbox. For each segment of a session, your facilitation plan should include what the group will talk about, and which method you will use to guide them through it.

Another advantage of this approach is that it gives you a visual reminder to incorporate variety into your sessions. If your methodology column on your facilitation plan says "discuss" beside every agenda item, you will know at a glance that there is likely too much talking and not enough moving around in your design. Sometimes meetings go off the rails simply out of boredom; as a conversation progresses over a long time, it can easily meander off track. If, however, you design conversations to be tightly focused and brief before moving on to a different modality, such as mapping an issue visually or working kinaesthetically with sticky notes or puzzle pieces, you are likely to keep the energy high and the momentum moving forward.

Plan in chunks

It is likely evident by now that another of my hacks to stay on track is to plan meetings in discrete chunks. Let's explore our car-buying example further. One chunk of the meeting could be about generating ideas of possible models of car. The next could be about identifying criteria to help narrow down the options. A third could involve applying those criteria to our possibilities to get us to a short list. What is key here is that each chunk has its own purpose. Knowing the overall goal, especially in longer sessions, may not be enough to stay on track towards it. Designing in chunks that each have a clear objective or mini-purpose can help you construct the path toward and then guard the achievement of the overall purpose. It also helps to know which of the chunks is especially important, so that you will know where to trim and where not to once the session is underway. I think of these chunks as blazes on a trail toward the ultimate destination: even if the group gets off the trail for a short time, you can look for the next blaze up ahead and find your way back. The finish line is not always in sight, so we need a few markers along the way.

For example, I plan a full-day workshop in four ninety-minute chunks: before the morning break, between the break and lunch, between the lunch and the afternoon break, and between that break and the end of the day. Each of those four chunks would have its own mini-purpose. If necessary, depending on the complexity of the design, I could further subdivide those chunks into 30-minute blocks.

These two elements of maintaining a purpose-based facilitation design (i.e. attending to both content and experience and planning in chunks) are integrated in the Facilitation Planning Template. Taken together, they help to build a discipline of purpose-driven design that will stick in your mind as you head into the room.

One-Day Facilitation Plan

PURPOSE		
1a	30 mins	
1b	30 mins	90 mins
1c	30 mins	
BREAK	15 mins	
2a	30 mins	
2b	30 mins	90 mins
2c	30 mins	
LUNCH	30 mins	
3a	30 mins	
3b	30 mins	90 mins
3c	30 mins	
BREAK	15 mins	
4a	30 mins	
4b	30 mins	90 mins
4c	30 mins	

Facilitation Planning Template

Overall Purpose of the session:

Objectives for this section or "chunk"	Content: Topics to address	Experience/Methodology: Process, techniques or activities	Supplies needed	Approximate timing

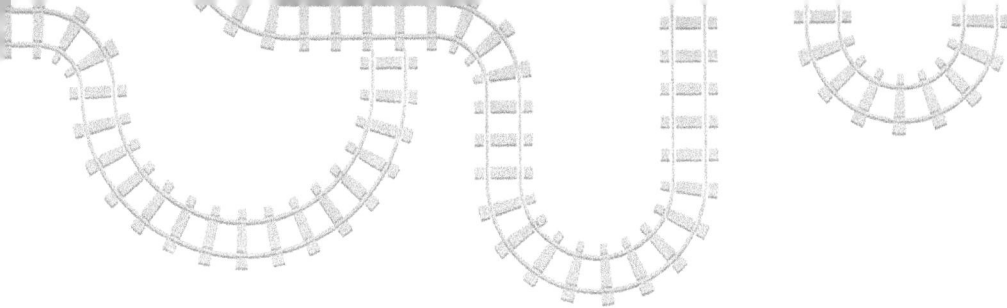

Place

	In advance ANTICIPATION	In the room AGILITY	Afterwards ABSORPTION
PEOPLE	**About you** **About others**	About you About others	About you About others
PURPOSE	**Clarify it** **Use it**	Clarify it Use it	Clarify it Use it
PLACE	**Leverage it** **Learn from it**	Leverage it Learn from it	Leverage it Learn from it
PROCESS	Script it Hold it loosely	Script it Hold it loosely	Script it Hold it loosely

The third element of anticipation to aid your advance preparation as a facilitator is place. Throughout, we will address place in two ways: the physical space in which a meeting occurs, and the vibe or dynamic occurring within that space once the group inhabits it. We will look at how to leverage and learn from the space by using it to further the achievement of the group's objectives.

LEVERAGE IT

The third dimension of readiness that can contribute preventatively to your agility at the front of the room is the room itself.

The physical space you are in will affect the work that gets done in that space.

If the space works well, your need to adapt will be far lower than if the venue is poorly suited to the activities happening within it. To illustrate, we will consider here how space can influence a session both positively and negatively.

Positive planning variable

The positive side of the importance of space is that creatively chosen venues can significantly enhance the quality of the work done in them. I once conducted a workshop with teachers on the value of incorporating local food into their schools. We held the event at a local farm, enjoying a walking tour of the farm on our break and feasting on a delicious lunch of products grown there. Do you think those teachers were more likely to embrace the concept of promoting local food than if we had held the same conversation in a generic boardroom?

This theme is reinforced by Scott Doorley and Scott Witthoft in their book *Making Space*.[39] We know from research on office design that our social environment plays a large role in our ability to concentrate, connect, create and stay motivated.[40] Why would the same not be true in a facilitated setting? Yet in a facilitated session, the effects of the space stack up quickly because the time spent in the space is usually shorter. All the more reason, then, to ensure that first impressions are positive and that the features of the space contribute to, rather than detract from, the achievement of the session's purposes.

Given the importance of space in shaping outcomes, facilitators should proactively take responsibility for selecting and using the venue as a planning variable to improve the quality of their session. As with relational currency above, when you make an effort to wow people, they are less likely to worry about other small glitches that may occur. And conversely, poorly chosen space can require you to be far more nimble in your facilitation to compensate for its flaws than you otherwise would have had to be.

Sometimes all that is required is remembering that you do have options when it comes to space selection. Just because you are facilitating a weekly

Space Planning Checklist

Whenever possible, I like to visit the space in advance or have someone send photos of the room. This helps determine its suitability and allows you to anticipate ways in which the space can add to or detract from the productivity of a session. This checklist will help determine if the space meets your needs and help eliminate surprises the day of the meeting.

Room availability

- ☐ Available for date and time of meeting
- ☐ Early access to room (i.e. to set up, put out material, test equipment)
- ☐ Extended access to room (i.e. if running late. Is the room booked for anything else?)
- ☐ When do we have to be out of the room?
- ☐ Other meetings or activities (i.e. construction) going on at same time or nearby
- ☐ Large space for participants and the activities planned (should have generous proportions rather than just big enough)
- ☐ Does the "vibe" of the room match the desired tone or content of the meeting?

Location and meeting room amenities

- ☐ On-site parking and the cost
- ☐ Washrooms close to meeting room
- ☐ Natural light
- ☐ Window shades to block the sun's glare
- ☐ Lights with dimmers
- ☐ Temperature control
- ☐ Room acoustics
- ☐ Coat racks and hangers

Equipment and supplies

- ☐ Projector, screen, speakers
- ☐ Wi-Fi available (What's the password?)
- ☐ Extension cords and power bars
- ☐ White board with dry-erase markers
- ☐ Blank walls that you can post things on
- ☐ Facilitation materials/supplies needed (i.e. tape, paper, markers, etc.)

Room set-up

- ☐ Room layout – determine the best layout for your meeting
- ☐ Who will set up the room and when?
- ☐ Everyone can see the screen/"working walls"
- ☐ Furniture that can be easily moved
- ☐ Extra table for facilitation supplies
- ☐ Extra table(s) for food an
- ☐ Pitchers of water and glasses
- ☐ Coffee maker and mugs
- ☐ Garbage and recycling bins
- ☐ Door stopper
- ☐ Directional signs with arrows pointing in different directions and labelled "meeting"

On-site contact for space related questions or problems (i.e. temperature adjustment, A/V equipment)

- ☐ Contact name and number for day of meeting
- ☐ Back-up person

team meeting, you do not have to conduct that meeting in the same room every week. Change it up! There is value in introducing an element of the unexpected.

As you will notice in the Space Planning Checklist[41], on the previous page, some features of the venue are more malleable than others. There is very little you can do about the amount of natural light in a space, but you can notice if there are blinds installed to address the glare at certain times of day. You can ask for the Wi-Fi password, but can't do much about poor cellular reception. You are unlikely to bring in your own whiteboards, but you can definitely supply your own markers if those aren't provided. Details matter. Control as many of them as you can.

Negative possibility

The negative side of the assertion that space affects what happens in it can unfortunately be illustrated by my own space-planning missteps. In my experience, inappropriate, ill-conceived space can undermine your effectiveness in two ways: by leading to a less successful meeting and by undermining the group's trust in your ability as a facilitator. The process goes poorly, and you look badly prepared. Consider the following examples (I wish I could tell you they're fictitious):

- An exercise where participants are asked to write on multiple flip charts posted around the room, yet the space is a former wine cellar with bumpy limestone walls, or a gallery where the walls have art bolted to them.

- A room so big that participants are too far away to read the words written on an easel, or so small that there is literally not enough space for people to get out of their chairs to conduct the participatory exercise.

- Chairs arranged in theatre-style rows bolted to the floor, making small group work a challenge.

- A creative visioning session in the most uninspiring room imaginable, which turns out to be the very space where people were informed about a significant downsizing initiative just the week before.

I have adjusted my preparation questions as a result of some of the experiences mentioned above. For example, instead of asking a client, "Is there wall space?" (a question I've learned that people hear as, "Are there walls?"), I now ask, "Is there smooth, blank wall space?"

When it comes to the space, there should be no surprises. Ask—even if it's a client with whom you have worked before, in a space you think you know. Provide a diagram of what furniture set up you need. Visit if you can. Request photos or perhaps even a live video tour if you can't.

LEARN FROM IT

Space selection also affords an opportunity for both you and your group to grow and learn. A poorly chosen venue will require you to adjust and adapt constantly to make things work. When well chosen, however, the venue can give you the tailwind you need to soar through the session with less effort and more energy.

Stretch the group

Venue selection provides an opportunity for you to leverage your knowledge of your people. I was once invited to facilitate an event that the client referred to as a "retreat getaway." She chose the venue, and it ended up being a private dining room in a members-only club. Participants were in jackets and dress pants. Not my idea of a retreat getaway, but she knew her people. For them, it was a big deal to get out of the office and for the men to remove their neckties. If you have a choice between booking a yurt in the woods and a corporate boardroom, know the style and tolerance of your group.

But what if my retreat getaway client might have actually *preferred* or done better by getting out in the country rather than going to the country club? Another aspect of preparing well as a nimble facilitator is deciding how far to stretch your group. Just how much of a departure from the norm— in terms of both place and process—would benefit the achievement of the group's purposes? This is another judgment call, but I would suggest keeping the following tips in mind:

- Incorporating some level of humour, playfulness and/or the unexpected can put people in a positive frame of mind and help them perform better on creative tasks.[42]

- Align your design choices with the culture and style of the group—with a bit of reach. If they are usually a pretty conservative bunch, bear in mind that their tolerance for change will likely be low. But perhaps they are craving something different without even realizing it—hence the reach. Don't pigeonhole them too tightly if what they might really need is to shake things up. An interesting venue is a low-risk way to introduce that possibility to them.

- Your choice of venue and activities should always be purposeful. (You knew I was going to say that, right?) If one of your aims is to push the group beyond its comfort zone so that it can become more innovative, then it makes sense to choose an unusual location or to introduce some activities that are a bit outside their norm. If, however, you are simply introducing a goofy activity because it appeals to you, with little connection to any objective of the session, people are likely to be more resistant to this unjustified experimentation.

Stretch yourself

Choosing a venue that is a bit of a stretch can also challenge you as the facilitator. Your choice of space should match your style enough that you can "pull it off" with authenticity. A tattooed, vegan yoga instructor will likely be able to walk a group through a guided meditation exercise in the woods with greater credibility than a slick corporate executive in a pencil skirt could. Again, pay attention to alignment between who you are and what you are proposing the group do—but leave space for a bit of a stretch. Habit can be an enemy of adaptability.[43] Trying something new gives us the adrenaline we need to perform at our best and makes us better at our craft, so don't be too quick to rule things out if they seem a bit uncomfortable.

Look for the sweet spot where your vibe and the group's norms intersect. If your style and your group's culture are so fundamentally different that you wonder why you were selected to run this meeting in the first place, then the overlap in preferences might be quite small. But if you can create a scenario where both you and the group are on your toes yet comfortable enough to feel safe enough to participate, you are likely setting the session up for success.

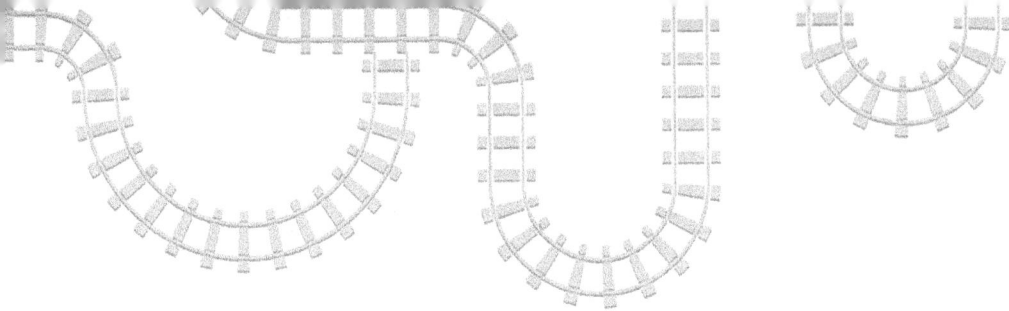

Process

	In advance ANTICIPATION	In the room AGILITY	Afterwards ABSORPTION
PEOPLE	About you About others	About you About others	About you About others
PURPOSE	Clarify it Use it	Clarify it Use it	Clarify it Use it
PLACE	Leverage it Learn from it	Leverage it Learn from it	Leverage it Learn from it
PROCESS	Script it Hold it loosely	Script it Hold it loosely	Script it Hold it loosely

Once you have built your own skills, clarified the purposes of the session and selected the venue, you are ready to begin crafting the specifics of your process design. This is the final dimension of preparation, and one that has enormous power to influence how nimble you will eventually need to be once you get into the room. Here, we find ourselves in the midst of a tension between scripting the session and holding that script loosely.

SCRIPT IT

Entire books have been devoted to the skill of facilitated process design— Ingrid Bens, Dorothy Strachan, Roger Schwarz, and Michael Wilkinson are just a few of my favourites among many authors who have written on this.[44]

I will focus on two specific considerations when crafting your facilitation script; alignment and level of detail. Both of these considerations will help you to put together a script that's strong and versatile. Next, we'll learn how to let go of this script that we've put so much work into! We'll look at two ways to loosen your grip on it, so that you can adapt to any scenario that comes your way.

Alignment between activity and intent

Here, we revisit in more detail a concept introduced earlier: the need to align your choice of activity with the intent of that chunk of the meeting. Previously, our focus was on ensuring that each segment of a meeting has a clear objective. This time, we'll explore selecting activities that align with that objective, as a way to offset the need for facilitation agility.

Let's return to our car-buying example, and to the skill of anticipation. Imagine if I said to a group, "Over the next 90 minutes, our task is to narrow down our vehicle choice from our short list of four possibilities to one winning model." Fair enough—the objective is clear. But then continue to hold this scenario in your imagination as I say, "We're going to brainstorm about this. Please write your ideas on sticky notes. There are no bad ideas. This is a 'blue sky' exercise. Let's get as many ideas as possible up on the wall in five minutes. Go!"

There would likely be some confused looks in the room. Some participants would compliantly get on with the task. Others would disengage and check their phones. Likely others would put their hand up and ask a question about the process, while others just grumble in bewilderment. In that moment, because of a misalignment between the objective of the session (i.e. decision making) and the intent of the activity (i.e. idea generation), I have lost the trust of the group and momentum has stalled. Both of these problems now require me to be more agile than if things had gone smoothly. This may seem like I'm jumping ahead to tips for 'in the room,' but in fact this is a problem that can be traced directly back to poor process planning.

Each facilitation tool in your toolbox is best used in a particular scenario. Brainstorming is best for idea generation. Dot voting is best for gauging comparative support between options. Spectrum exercises indicate preferences and the level of consensus in the room. Used for these purposes, these activities can be highly effective. If there is a mismatch between the intent of an activity and its usage, however, a session can veer off the rails very quickly. It's like picking up a screwdriver to saw a piece of wood in two. Choose the right tool for the job.

Level of detail

The second design consideration that can help avoid the need for adjusting on the fly is to develop a facilitation plan that contains the appropriate level of detail. In an earlier section on knowing yourself, I referred to personal variations in people's comfort level regarding the level of detail needed in an agenda. I return to that topic here, to help you combine that personal preference with the level of detail required for you to be both well prepared and agile in the room. This really is a balancing act. Too much detail will make it difficult for you to hold your script loosely and maintain the flexibility needed to be responsive to participants. Too little, and you will be surprised by things that should not have been surprising if you had planned more thoroughly. This dynamic is often further complicated by the expectations of the client or sponsor, who might want a detailed agenda provided to participants in advance.

Charles Perrow in his book *Normal Accidents* describes the conditions under which accidents happen: when a system is both complex (i.e. interactions occur in unfamiliar, unplanned or unexpected ways) and "tightly coupled" which means activities must occur in a set sequence with little time lag or variation or opportunity for substitution.[45] Applied to facilitation, complexity is inevitable, but tight coupling is not. Accidents are less likely to happen when some slack, redundancy, or improvisation is built into the system.

Picture the following scenario: you are handed an agenda with times devoted to each topic. The times are noted to the minute; at 10:12 we'll do this and at 10:27 we'll move on to something else. Imagine how you feel at 10:16 when the group is still on the first item. Is your blood pressure rising? Are you having trouble concentrating on the meeting content? Yet if you had not been given such a precise agenda, would you be worried about going four minutes over the original time? Not likely. The facilitator might feel comfortable with that level of detail, but as a participant it is more likely to raise your stress level rather than lowering it.

My recommendation is to keep the following principles in mind as you design a facilitated process:

- The public-facing agenda should be less detailed than your personal facilitation plan. Participants do not require detailed descriptions of your timing or instructions or supply list, but you do. The key components of a meeting agenda are the purpose, location, start and end times, whether participants can expect to be fed, and any preparation. That's all. If you provide participants with more detailed times for each activity, you constrain yourself unnecessarily. When you are unable to match those times exactly (which is inevitable), you create stress for your participants and yourself.

- Surprises can be terrific when planned for participants in a session, but they are less welcome when experienced by the person planning the session. Work to minimize them for yourself and for the client by covering enough detail.

- The more detailed your facilitation plan (see the Facilitation Planning Template in the earlier chapter on Purpose), the more difficult it may be for you to deviate from it. In some cases, such as when it comes to staying focused on the purpose, this rigidity is a benefit. But often it is not. It can prevent you from being responsive to what is happening in the room, causing you to defend your beautifully crafted design instead of adjusting to what the group really needs. The meeting becomes about you rather than about them. Instead, build an intention to stay flexible right into your design, by using a technique such as the one I am about to describe.

HOLD IT LOOSELY

Now that you have your facilitation plan in hand, you need to step back from it. Here are two techniques to help you get some new perspective on your process, thereby using it as a guide but not a script when you eventually walk into the room.

Multiple scenarios

One way to design your facilitated session with built-in flexibility is to plan deliberately for multiple scenarios. Assume that things will go differently than planned rather than being surprised when they do. This technique really puts your skills of anticipation to the test. Here's how it works:

Design a chunk of your meeting. (Notice how I said "design" it—having an agenda alone is not enough, remember? And only a chunk, for now). Imagine how your process might play out. Picture yourself asking that question or describing that activity. Perhaps even speak the instructions out loud. What are the participants likely to say or produce in response? If they do, what would you say next? Run through the script in your mind. Will that line of questioning take you where you want to go? Make it flow beautifully.

Then let it go. Go back and redesign that same chunk of the meeting a whole different way. Choose a different activity to reach the same purpose. Imagine a different response to your question, one that takes the group in a completely new direction. What would you say then?

The point of this approach is not to "get it right." It is highly unlikely that Plan A will unfold as envisioned, and when it doesn't, Plan B is not likely to happen either. But by inviting your brain to consider more than one scenario in detail in advance, it is now readier than it otherwise would have been to cope with Plan C when that's what actually occurs. Two things happen: you are more thoroughly prepared because you have dug deeper into your facilitation toolbox and discovered you have several options of how to accomplish a goal, and you are more agile because you have taught yourself how to hold your carefully constructed script loosely. Maybe even to scrap it. All without sacrificing the purpose of the session.

Planning for multiple scenarios not only helps you envision adjusting to multiple answers to a given question, but it is also useful in crafting process designs that flex with varied group sizes (see the Planning for Multiple Scenarios Template in the online toolkit). Although at times you can accurately predict how many people will attend a meeting, there are many situations when the size of the gathering is unpredictable, such as with public hearings or open-invitation town hall meetings. In that case, designing multiple scenarios moves from a planning discipline to a practical necessity. I find it helpful to plan for a small group (perhaps under 10 people), a medium-sized group (10-20), a large group (20-75) and a very large group (75+). It is rare that you need to have a plan for all four sizes, but it's worth getting good at it, just in case.

Manage mojo

Another process-related strategy that will prevent the group going off the rails before you even walk into the room as a facilitator is "managing the mojo." You have an opportunity to decide in advance how you will work with the energy of the group to accomplish their objectives. Responding willingly and intentionally to the group's energy level can help you loosen your grip on your script.

Most of us know the feeling of the 4 p.m. lull. (Sometimes it hits at 1:30!) We desperately need a nap. Or caffeine. Or a lot of sugar.

Did you know that this lull is grounded in science? In his book *When*, Daniel Pink shows us that our moods and cognitive abilities follow a rigorous pattern. Across continents and time zones, everyone experiences the day in three stages: a peak, a trough, and a rebound (not necessarily in that order).[46] His findings are echoed by Kristen Hansen's work on the neuroscience of leadership. She writes, "We typically get to a point where our prefrontal cortex is depleted at about 3 o'clock in the afternoon. Although this is a generalisation, it's a pretty reasonable one. Up to 40% of every group I have ever trained experiences this afternoon dip sometime between 2-3p.m. It is not a great time to start a new project, because our prefrontal cortex feels like it's running out of gas. We can feel tired, less creative, and experience more mental blockages."[47]

Canadian scientist Martha Lenio refers to the same phenomenon in a story about her Mars simulation expedition.[48] NASA was researching how to support teams on extended, isolated space missions. NASA knew that without fail, teams' energy and cooperative spirit tend to lag about two-thirds of the way through a mission. This proved to be true on the mission commanded by Lenio as well. She explains it visually, drawing on work from John H. Rohrer[49] and Robert Bechtel and Amy Berning.[50] As you can see from the diagram, adapted from their work and hers, all teams hit the dip. Some head steadily back up to a more positive state near the end of their assignment and others claw their way back, but they do get there.

Design for the Dip

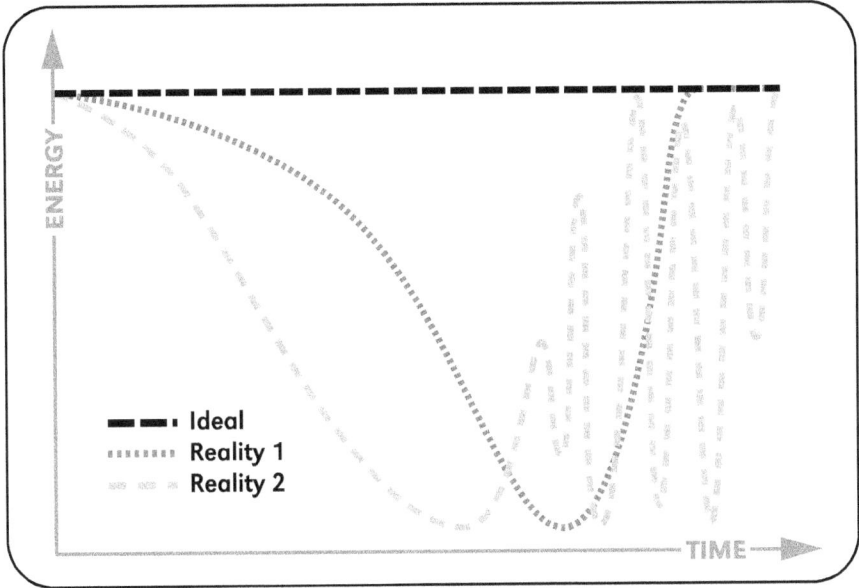

This pattern is true over the course of a day, a week (Wednesday is known as Hump Day for that reason), a space mission, or a life—perhaps mid-life crises would be better described as mid-life energy dips.[51]

It is not surprising then that a similar energy pattern is evident in facilitated events. As a facilitator who wants to pre-empt the need to bring things back on track, you need to "design for the dip"—both in yourself and in your participants. The facilitator is responsible for managing the energy in the room, and because energy levels follow predictable patterns, this energy management task begins at the planning stage. The first step is anticipating the lull. If you are managing a day-long event, it will come in the early to mid-afternoon. If it's a week, expect it on Wednesday.

The next step is to decide what to do about it. You have three basic choices. One is to ignore the dip. I would advise against that approach, as doing so entrenches your identity as the Oblivious Facilitator. The second is to give in to it. Let people rest. Give them a passive, non-demanding task in the afternoon such as watching a video. Or even schedule an extended break and reconvene later on. The final option is to counteract the energy dip with a lively, dynamic activity in your plan—perhaps a field trip or an active assignment or an unexpected guest—accompanied by a highly energetic presence on your part, as demonstrated by your voice, countenance and body language.

Rather than heavy-handed scripting in response to anticipated lulls, let the energy patterns in the room lead you into a more intuitive, responsive facilitation approach.

This predictable energy pattern is why I find it puzzling to have keynote speakers open conferences. Participants arrive energized and ready to engage, and almost invariably they are asked to sit passively and listen. Would it not be better to channel that energy into productive activity in the morning and invite the speaker to inject her expertise in other ways later on in the day?

You are also the guardian of your own personal energy as the facilitator, and you can plan similarly for your own lulls. For instance, if you tend toward introversion and find yourself drained by the uninterrupted presence of others, then you may need to remind yourself to take breaks during the scheduled breaks rather than getting drawn into conversations with people during those times. Hide in the bathroom stall and recharge your personal batteries! Or get the group busy doing something in the afternoon rather than designing an activity that requires you to be at your most articulate and energetic at that time.

The point here is that the energy dip is real. If you ignore it, you risk losing the group and your need for facilitation agility increases. If, however, you deliberately plan for it, you can help the group stay on track and reduce the need to adapt on the fly. Overall, you are more likely to perform well and you'll likely increase your currency in the eyes of your participants.[52]

AGILITY IN ADVANCE

When you pay attention in advance to these four domains of preparation—person, purpose, place and process—you offset the need to be nimble in the room as a result of causes that could reasonably have been predicted and avoided. Ideally, all four Ps will be shored up and aligned so that you are ready on all levels. The purpose is clear, the venue is well-suited to achieving that purpose, you are personally in a state of balance between being deeply grounded and highly aware of your surroundings, and you have planned a process that is both robust and flexible. It sounds like a tall order, and it is. You do what you can in advance, and then you loosen your grip. It's showtime!

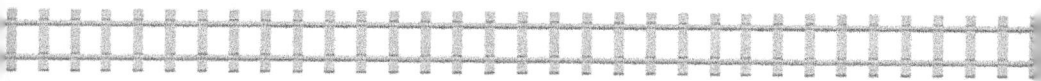

In the room: Agility

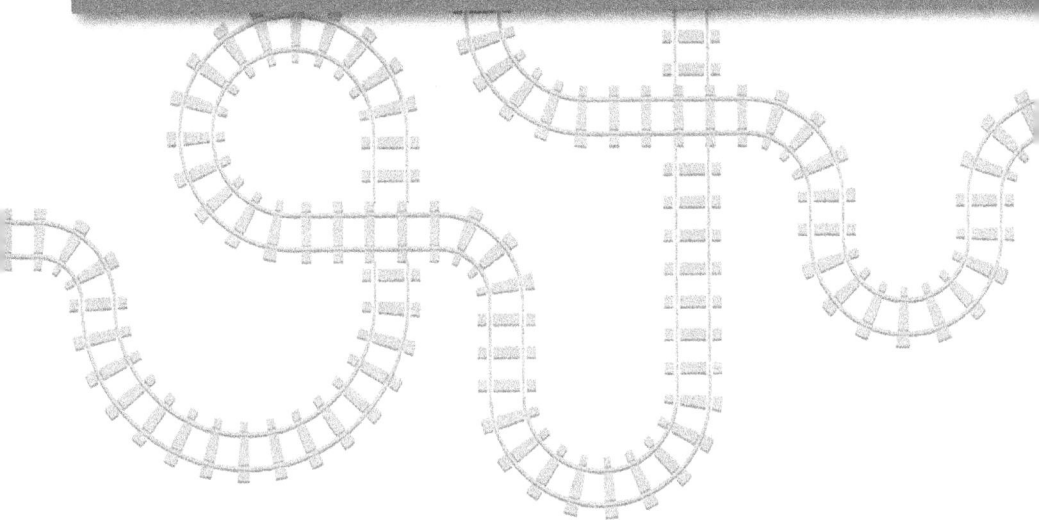

I suspect many readers will have picked up this book looking for this section. What to do when things in the room go differently than you expected, and you are put in a position of having to adjust on the fly.

Preparation is critically important to offset the need to be nimble in the room; so much so that I have devoted roughly half of this book to it. But as previously noted, your design and techniques may only represent 60-70% of what actually happens in the room, even when you are very well prepared. Our anticipation skills will never prove to be 100% accurate. And let's be honest—often we are not as well-prepared as we would like to be.

This means that we need strategies for coping effectively with whatever happens in the room. I call this building our "rapid recovery" skills. These are what help us both to keep things on course and to get them back on track quickly when they threaten to derail.

The level of seriousness of the derailment can vary. Sometimes it may be as simple as experiencing silence in response to a question you thought would generate lively discussion. Or hearing responses to that same question that take the conversation in a direction quite different from the one you expected, resulting in you having to adjust your subsequent question. Often a group exercise brings issues to the surface that you couldn't have guessed in advance, and you need to respond to those issues rather than to the ones you thought would come up. It sounds simple, but if you have built a tight, linear design, even moderate detours can take you well off course by the end of the meeting.

Although the specifics of the situation can vary widely, there are some mindsets, skills and behaviours that will help you adapt to whatever you face from the front of the room. As before, we will focus on the four Ps—people, purpose, place and process. Within people, again including ourselves and others, we will break it down into fuel and focus. Within purpose, we will highlight the importance of both clarifying purpose, by keeping it visible to ourselves and to the group, and then using that purpose to decide if we are on track and if in fact we want to stay on that track. Our discussion of place will help us to leverage and learn from the physical venue and its vibe, through ensuring that the room is well stocked and does not itself generate any surprises, and also through developing structures that help us pay attention to and understand the dynamics that may be emerging. Finally, the section on process again addresses how to script a session thoroughly and then to hold your script loosely. It offers 18 practical tips for how to navigate the group, and yourself, through experiences of feeling lost or stuck.

People

	In advance **ANTICIPATION**	In the room **AGILITY**	Afterwards **ABSORPTION**
PEOPLE	About you About others	About you About others	About you About others
PURPOSE	Clarify it Use it	Clarify it Use it	Clarify it Use it
PLACE	Leverage it Learn from it	Leverage it Learn from it	Leverage it Learn from it
PROCESS	Script it Hold it loosely	Script it Hold it loosely	Script it Hold it loosely

In the room, you need to pay attention to people. This involves more than "reading the room"—it means being deliberately attentive to both yourself and to others. We will explore each in turn, looking at fuel and focus as key concepts.

ABOUT YOU

If advance preparation involves increasing your self-awareness, then in the room is your opportunity to apply that knowledge. As a facilitator, your main tool is yourself. Assuming you have done your preventative maintenance ahead of time, your job now is to maintain a calm, helpful presence. You are the group's navigator and chaperone. No traveller wants a safari guide who's edgy and unsure of the way!

Like a high-performance athlete, you need to trust your training for the task at hand. But you also need to be at your best on game day. Matt Church is often heard saying, "Your state is more important than your script." Particularly in the hours before a big facilitation event, make sure you look after yourself.

Fuel

My number one facilitation tip: Go to bed early the night before.

The most important thing you can do is to show up well-rested and sharp. Facilitation agility requires mental clarity and energy. A sluggish, foggy brain will not get you there.

There is now little doubt that sleep improves cognition, while a lack of sleep impairs it. Sleep is known to strengthen many aspects of neural processing, including insight formation, novel language perception, visual discrimination and motor skills. Consider how useful each of these skills is to a facilitator. Conversely, sleep deprivation causes profound impairments in cognitive and behavioural performance, including 36% more serious errors among medical interns on a "traditional schedule" compared to those getting more sleep.[53] According to a 2017 study, the UK is the world's most sleep-deprived nation, with Canada sitting at number three, and the USA sitting at number six. [54] We do not do well at this!

Other fundamentals of self-care critical to keeping you at the top of your facilitation game include hydration (be careful of talking too quickly as your caffeine intake climbs!), nutrition, exercise and following your morning routine. These may sound like basic tips, but there is a significant gap between what we know and what we do. For example, only 15% of Canadian adults are meeting current physical activity guidelines,[55] so clearly this is advice we struggle to follow. Common sense is not that common, apparently.

Some of these disciplines happen before you arrive at the session, but staying fuelled up needs attention even once the session is underway.

First, you need to gain the trust of the group right from the start. We have already highlighted the importance of building rapport as people arrive. Now that they are in their seats and you have their full attention, you have a very short time to convince them to decide to trust you. As the saying goes, "You never get a second chance to make a first impression." Start strong. Please don't say, "I'm happy to be here" unless you can pull it off authentically. Help your participants connect with the purpose of the session. Get them excited. Demonstrate you have skills, insight, energy and a plan. Show the group you are worthy of their confidence, right from your opening statement, so that they will be willing to entrust their time and their objectives to your leadership for the rest of the session. Their trust will give you energy. The opposite is also true. Mutiny in the room requires you to be incredibly nimble under pressure. Building a loyal team around you is a preventative facilitation strategy that works, and it starts in the first thirty seconds of a meeting.[56]

Then, as the session unfolds, pay attention to your self-talk. Make sure that inner voice is behaving more like a cheerleader than a critic.[57] You have been cultivating the ability to enhance the positive in your preparation; now is the time to pay attention to that affirming inner monologue and banish any recriminations that might try to creep into your mind as the session progresses. Brené Brown calls these negative thoughts your "gremlins"—don't listen to them.[58] Instead, engage in what Donald Schon refers to as "reflection-in-action"—notice what is happening, consider it and respond.[59] Remember, things going differently than expected is what we expect to happen. Celebrate your new ability to embrace that truth.

One other reminder related to self-talk: we tend to be so invested in our carefully crafted facilitated session that we think things are about us, when in fact they have nothing to do with us at all. It's a classic example of the spotlight effect; we overestimate how much other people are noticing us, even when we are in the spotlight! Responsibility for the outcomes of a facilitated conversation ultimately rests with the participants. Most of the dynamics you notice in the room predate your arrival and will continue long after you are gone. Keep your role in perspective.

Finally, remember that your obligation to monitor your own state of being continues right through to the end of the meeting. Beware of your tendencies when weariness sets in (remember that dip in energy I described earlier?) as we rarely facilitate well when we are not at our best. I remember attending a debrief session based on a popular temperament assessment tool. The consultant wisely phrased her feedback on the more undesirable aspects of each personality type as "Here is how this type behaves when her needs aren't being met." Watch for this in yourself at the end of the day. When I am tired near the end of a session, I become hyper-focused on achieving the objectives, usually talking more than I should and becoming too directive of the group. We all need extra support when we are vulnerable—it's why we need pre-cut vegetables in the refrigerator at 4 p.m. so we don't just eat the leftover cheesecake! Make sure your needs are being met, and when they aren't, be careful the needs of the group don't suffer as a result. Do what you need to do to ensure your fuel tank is full when it counts.

Focus

Another element of self-management on the day of a facilitated session involves consciously directing your focus. This strategy involves both positive and negative aspects: minimizing unhelpful distractions and deliberately choosing to direct your attention toward inputs that will accelerate your performance.

Australian communication expert and thought leader Jane Anderson coaches her clients to put away their cell phones, even as much as 48 hours before a high-stakes session, in order to focus their attention uncompromisingly on the task at hand.[60] While that might seem extreme, there is increasing evidence in the productivity literature of the importance of managing your focus rather than managing your time.[61] In *Deep Work*, Cal Newport argues that we are rapidly forgetting the value of going deep. Uninterrupted, distraction-free and carefully directed concentration produces extremely valuable output, and is a deliberate practice that needs to be cultivated in order to be effective.[62] As per the Roman philosopher Seneca, "There is never a time when a new distraction will not show up."[63]

Another important aspect of controlling our focus is managing our emotions. Psychologist Victor Johnston describes emotions as "discriminant hedonic amplifiers"—in other words, they are attention magnets, drawing our attention toward certain issues and away from others.[64] Self-regulation is essential at the front of the room. Common strategies that build your capacity for emotional regulation mirror those already discussed, including sleep, exercise, time in nature, journaling, and plugging leaks in our attention by minimizing distractions. Another protective tactic is to leave open space in your schedule, especially right before a critical session. Doing so creates mind space and breathing room. You can also pay particular attention to things that trigger strong emotional reactions in you and do what's needed to avoid those triggers when you are heading into an important session. You need a plan for how you will handle triggering behaviours that might emerge within the session itself. Lowering unhelpful stress is fundamental to optimal performance.

Once you are ready to turn your attention to the details of the session at hand, pull out your facilitation plan (prepared in advance, of course!) Read over your script, practice your opening, *then set it aside*. It's time to loosen your grip on it. Instead of poring over its details just ahead of a session, consider preparing yourself physically instead. In her book *Presence*, Amy Cuddy affirms, "...preparation is obviously important, but at some point, you must stop preparing content and start preparing mindset."[65] She affirms that our body speaks to our mind. Clench and unclench your fists, for example, as a reminder of your need to honour your preparation without clinging too tightly to it. Adopt a power pose (think Wonder Woman). Pay attention to your posture: stand taller, with your head and shoulders back. These may seem like small techniques at first, but they yield powerful results in helping us to be fully present. Cuddy describes presence as that self-assured enthusiasm that allows us to be attuned to and able to express our truth.[66] That's the space we need to inhabit as we walk into the room.

Another way to up your game before walking in the room is by setting an intention or focus. We know from athletic training that your mind impacts how your muscles activate. Did you know that when you think about a particular muscle as you work out, it gets stronger than it would without that mental focus?[67] The same can be true in other realms of learning. Select a facilitation approach or situation that will be your focus for improvement this time around. Perhaps you want to do one thing that was not in your facilitation plan, in response to a need in the room. Or maybe you want to focus on conveying complete outward calm when something unexpected happens. Your dexterity in handling that particular scenario will undoubtedly increase simply by virtue of deciding to pay it deliberate attention today.

You may also need to be deliberate about what you will *not* focus on. In a recent facilitated session, I caught myself straying into mental problem-solving—listening to participants' ideas and trying to put the group's puzzle together. I started getting stressed about not being able to see a solution. This is unhelpful behaviour as a facilitator, as it pulled me away from being fully present in the moment and took up valuable mind space at a time when I needed every bit of brain capacity I could muster. Keep your focus only on the task at hand, even if that means resisting what might feel like worthy distractions.

Fear is an enemy of adaptability.[68]

One additional tip for maintaining a full presence, particularly if you are feeling at all nervous, is to commit to staying curious.

When we are under stress, our brains switch into fight-or-flight mode. In that state, we struggle to learn new things or activate our memory, and we tend to entrench.[69] It's the equivalent of being flat-footed instead of keeping your knees soft on a tennis court or football field: you're frozen rather than ready to move. Curiosity can help. If things unfold differently than you anticipated, notice it and adjust with a sense of interest, learning and wonder rather than frustration or panic. If you walked into the room expecting the meeting to go differently than planned, and it does, then things are happening right in line with your expectations. You're fine!

ABOUT OTHERS

Fuel

Just as you need to be powered up for your facilitation duties, your participants need fuel too. Some of the responsibility to ensure they get it falls to you. You don't want a session to go off the rails simply because your participants are hungry or need some fresh air! Pay attention to their needs. Nourish them well. Take breaks often.

Not only will meeting their basic needs for food, daylight and rest help participants' minds stay sharp in the room, but it will also bolster their confidence in you. Trust is in the details. If the logistics of an event run seamlessly and people's energy is managed well throughout, their focus can stay on the task at hand. If, however, the basics of event planning are not handled well, it is not a big stretch for participants to question whether you can be trusted to handle bigger issues. Right now, you may be thinking, "But event planning is not my job…!" Perhaps not, but as the facilitator, you are the face of the event to participants. If the details of event planning are not attended to in advance, you will be starting from a deficit position from the participants' perspective when you take the stage. One specific way to demonstrate this is to be a trustworthy time manager. If you say lunch is at noon, it should be at noon or slightly earlier, never later. Then, when you are punctual, you can expect your participants to be as well. You have the credibility to say, "I have committed to getting you out of here by 4 p.m. sharp, but in order for me to do that, I need you all back from lunch and ready to go by 1 p.m. sharp."

You can also keep your participants well-fuelled in the room by feeding their imaginations. Incorporate variety into your facilitation design. Surprise people. Delight them. Get them up and moving. By keeping people energized and purposefully engaged, you once again mitigate the risk of things going off the rails. People will be more willing to follow your script if it's an engrossing one.

You may not always get to choose the venue, but you can still have a lot of control over how it is used to energize a group. I was once asked to speak at an international conference that was being held in the Caribbean. It was pretty unusual for a conference to be held in that location and even more unusual for me to attend, so you can imagine my excitement! White sand, crystal-clear sea, picturesque palm trees…I was all hyped up to take advantage of the opportunity of working in such a beautiful setting.

However, when I arrived, I discovered that the entire conference was being held indoors in a large conference facility on the island. The building itself had beautiful parts, but the places that we were being asked to run these workshops in were generic, interior, basement, windowless hotel rooms. They had absolutely no personality at all. No view even of the palm trees, despite the ocean being literally 500 metres from where we were meeting. It felt like being in transit in an airport.

In that meeting it became even more important for me to give people breaks. I redesigned my session to give people a sense of place and a reminder of where we were. It was beautiful outside, and for those of us living through long winters and cold climates, that was especially frustrating. Because I was attuned to that frustration (partly due to feeling it myself!) I was able to leverage that awareness and make use of where we actually were. We took longer breaks to give people a chance to get outside, and shifted one of the activities to an outdoor walkabout. These breaks weren't only to recharge our batteries, but also designed to be a reminder of the importance of place itself.

The fact that the meeting was being held in the Caribbean should have, and could have, been a positive feature of that conference. And yet it ended up being treated simply as a generic setting that was in fact more expensive for most participants to reach. As unfair as it may be, don't let your own reputation carry the cost for mistakes in event planning. Do something about it.

Focus

In addition to keeping participants well-fuelled in the room, it is also your responsibility to manage their focus. Distraction undermines productivity. Here are three tips for ensuring a group keeps their attention on-task during a session:

1. Refuse to let yourself get distracted, even if the group does. Remember that you are the guardian of the purpose and the process. Fulfil that role faithfully, even if the group's attention is faltering. Draw their attention back to the task at hand, and to the reasons for it.

2. Provide clear opportunities for participants to attend to other matters. When people know a break is coming, they will be more likely to wait for these times to focus on outside concerns. Be sure you have alerted them to the points in the day when checking their messages will be

entirely appropriate. (And remember what I said about keeping them energized and engaged? Do that too. No one should look at their phone out of boredom during one of your meetings.)

3. Practice discernment regarding when to let the group deviate and when to insist they remain on the original track. When a group's focus shifts away from the original purpose or activity, you need to decide on the fly whether that unexpected detour is, in fact, likely to be more productive than the original script. Not sure? Ask the group. If opinions are mixed as to the relevance of the deviation, offer to spend 10 more minutes on it, then move on.

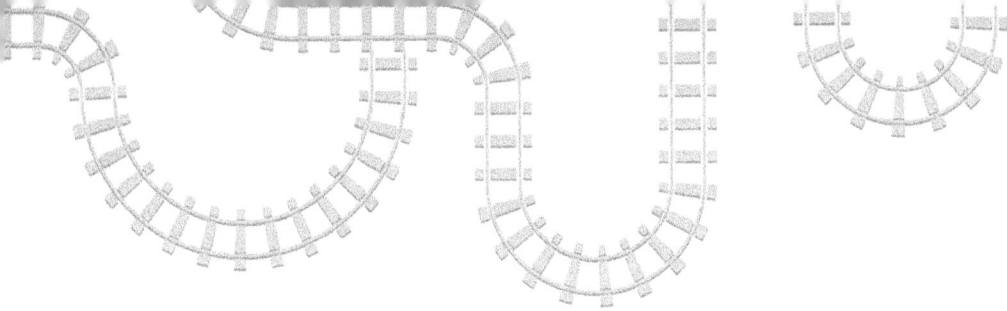

Purpose

	In advance **ANTICIPATION**	In the room **AGILITY**	Afterwards **ABSORPTION**
PEOPLE	About you About others	About you About others	About you About others
PURPOSE	Clarify it Use it	**Clarify it Use it**	Clarify it Use it
PLACE	Leverage it Learn from it	Leverage it Learn from it	Leverage it Learn from it
PROCESS	Script it Hold it loosely	Script it Hold it loosely	Script it Hold it loosely

The purpose is the standard by which to gauge whether or not a group is on track. It is also the key tool with which to keep things on track in the room. This happens by ensuring that the purpose is clear, and then employed. A tool is of little use if it stays in the toolbox!

CLARIFY IT

The substance of the purpose needs to be agreed upon and kept at the forefront of people's minds during the session.

Keep it visible to you

When you review your facilitation plan before walking into the room, focus on the purpose. Highlight it in your notes. Remind yourself of the overall intention of the session and the objectives of each chunk within it, both substantively and experientially. Keeping the purpose in the forefront of your mind is far more critical than memorizing the details of each activity or scripting each introduction. Guard your mind space and fill it with what is truly important.

One of my best reminders of the importance of keeping purpose in mind came from the most mundane of places—the grocery store. As I walked around stocking up on supplies, I noticed a mother pushing a grocery cart with a screaming toddler sitting inside. I'm always very sympathetic to people who are going through those kind of episodes, because I've been there. As she walked past, I could hear her saying, "We're almost home, Jessica… We're almost home. It's okay Jessica. We're almost home."

A few minutes later I found myself behind that same mother, still with the screaming toddler, in the lineup at the checkout. As the mother was unpacking her trolley, the child tried to reach for a candy. "No, Chloe. You can't have that."

And then it dawned on me. Chloe was the name of the child. The mother's name was Jessica, and those soothing words I'd heard earlier were being said to herself.

This incredible mother was exhausted and hating the current moment, but she knew that the best way to get out of the grocery store was to keep her eye on the prize. Even as things threatened to go off the rails, she kept herself focused by repeating her mantra of self-support and encouragement. The purpose of your facilitation session is a bit like that. The facilitator has to keep a running soundtrack in her mind saying, "This is what it's for. This is what I have to remember." Even in the midst of all the potential distractions or detours, keeping your purpose in mind will keep your session on track.

Keep it visible to the group

It is important that the purpose has buy-in from participants. If they are not invested in accomplishing the stated purpose, or perhaps not even in agreement with it, they will not join you in your mission to keep the group on track toward its achievement.

Ideally, the purpose would have been co-created with some of the participants in the first place or at least have been vetted with the group in advance. Either way, you are wise to confirm or refine the purpose at the start of a session so that people are contentedly moving in the same direction. Going off the rails is problematic, but travelling on completely different tracks toward multiple destinations is worse.

Once the purpose is confirmed, make it visible to everyone. Writing it on large paper on the wall is usually easiest, as doing so allows you to incorporate any last-minute changes in wording, but it is also possible to put it on a slide or in a handout. Whatever the format, the purpose should be accessible to participants throughout the session so that they, like you, can use it as a touchstone.

USE IT

Once the purpose has been confirmed and made visible, it is important to make use of it as the session unfolds.

Check we're on track

The purpose of the session is the standard against which you and the participants assess whether the process is on track. It is, therefore, good practice to draw people's attention back to it periodically, as a check-in for forward progress.

But what happens when making progress does not feel like forward motion? Sometimes we need to go sideways or even backwards to reach a destination. Often the scenery does not look familiar. Perhaps there are few landmarks along the way to reassure us that we are almost there. That is when the 'facilitator as calm guide' becomes an important role to play. You need to be able to trust the process and the group enough to navigate people confidently through unfamiliar territory, always with the purpose as your North Star. Sometimes that requires reassuring the group that you can still see the destination and the pathway to it, even when they cannot.

This is the moment when you will experience the importance of having clarified the purpose with the group. Draw on your shared picture of what the desired destination looks like, so you will know once you are there.

But what if your sightlines to the purpose are obscured too? Stay tuned. We are almost at the section on Process in the room, and it's full of useful tips to clear the fog.

Decide whether to switch tracks

We have noted that your primary filter for deciding if a detour is productive or not is discerning whether it is likely to move the group toward its intended purpose. But sometimes the purpose itself needs to shift, or it becomes clear that a group's multiple purposes are actually working at cross-purposes with each other. Even in those cases, the original purpose is your key tool. Hold it up to the group as a reminder of their original intention, mirroring back to them your observation that they appear now to be heading toward a different destination. Taking a few minutes as a group to decide whether the destination has now changed is always time well spent. If you are on the wrong train, usually the quickest way to the right one is to get off, rather than continuing further in the wrong direction. Your job as the facilitator is to help the group "fail fast"—to help them see clearly what is happening and to make a decision about where they want to go next. The purpose is theirs—so too is responsibility for revising it when necessary.

If, however, the detour is not worthy of a change in purpose, you may want to use a variation of what is traditionally known as a "Parking Lot," where items are captured to be dealt with later. In my experience, too often the Parking Lot can become the Cemetery, where ideas go to die! One way to breathe new life into an old technique is to rename or repurpose it. Call it the "Follow-up board" and list items alongside to indicate who/how/when follow up will occur. Note that if the group cannot quickly identify those next steps, the idea is likely not worth recording at this time.

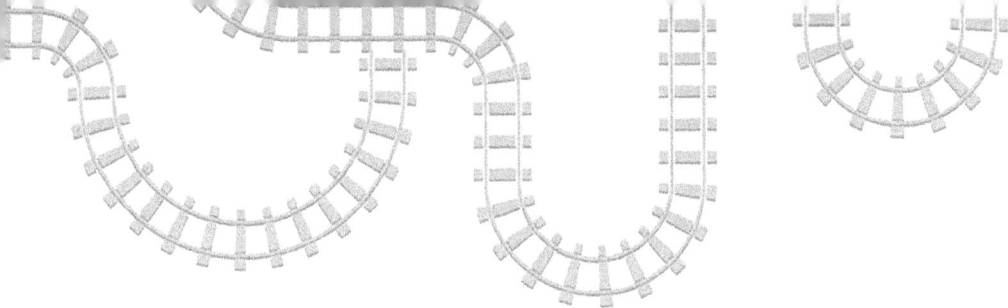

Place

	In advance **ANTICIPATION**	In the room **AGILITY**	Afterwards **ABSORPTION**
PEOPLE	About you About others	About you About others	About you About others
PURPOSE	Clarify it Use it	Clarify it Use it	Clarify it Use it
PLACE	Leverage it Learn from it	**Leverage it** **Learn from it**	Leverage it Learn from it
PROCESS	Script it Hold it loosely	Script it Hold it loosely	Script it Hold it loosely

Place in this context refers both to the venue and to the vibe in the room. Leveraging and using place means both paying attention to it and drawing on it as a resource throughout your facilitated session.

LEVERAGE IT

No surprises

Remember that when it comes to the meeting space, there should be no surprises. The key tip here is to arrive early or to make sure you have someone on your team who does. Why? Because, as I have already said, trust is in the details.

Community engagement expert Kate Bishop[70] shares a story of convening a public meeting over a contentious neighbourhood issue. She arrived to discover that the signage had advertised an incorrect start time, such that residents began arriving earlier than planned, expecting the meeting to begin before the team was set up. Then more people arrived. And still more. The coffee wasn't ready. They ran out of cups. The rented furniture was dusty. The room was overcrowded. How nimble do you think the facilitator had to be when that meeting started? She was digging herself out of a hole with an angry crowd before even opening her mouth. As one irritated participant said, "If we can't even trust you to plan a meeting, how can we trust you to plan our neighbourhood?"

Notice that, strictly speaking, the signage, furniture and refreshments were not the facilitator's responsibility. But in the moment, the facilitator is the one who has to deal with the fallout if the event-planning details are not handled well. Imagine how much more smoothly that session would have gone if the room had been ready and welcoming when the neighbours arrived. And how much easier the facilitator's job would have been as a result.

I hope you can also see in this example the importance of thorough preparation in advance in offsetting the need for nimbleness once you get in the room. The practical details and the vibe need to be right. But sometimes things still fall apart, despite the best-laid plans. Here are some additional quick tips for coping with a room set-up that isn't working:

- Call in reinforcements. If you are in a hotel or conference space, for instance, there will likely be hospitality or A/V staff on site. Maybe you have a team with you or could call others in. Get them busy making things right so that you can turn your attention to your job.

- Treat your participants as guests, not hired help. Resist the temptation to put them to work. Instead, find them another spot to wait; offer them a drink; introduce them to one another; give them something to do that is related to preparing their minds for the session that is about to start. Try to transform their immediate experience into something unexpectedly pleasant or productive rather than drawing them into the scramble that you and your team are handling.

- Stay calm and candid. Be clear with people about what is happening. Acknowledge whatever the problematic issues are and outline the path you are following to solve them. Use your rapport-building skills to their fullest to help people empathize, without seeming flustered or incompetent. Remember, if they are allies, they are going to extend you more patience—so work to get them on your side, even when you are not at your best.

Well stocked

I encourage facilitators to think like party planners. When you send out an invitation to a party, you know to include key details such as the reason, the location, the time and date, the format, the dress code and maybe even information about what to bring. We do this so that guests can easily and comfortably participate. No one wants to show up at a masquerade ball without a costume, or a birthday party without a gift. In the meantime, the host is ensuring that the venue is fully ready for what is about to happen. No one would arrive at a wedding reception to discover unset tables and someone still arranging the flowers for the centrepieces! Similarly, when planning a meeting, it is in the facilitator's best interest to ensure that participants and the meeting space are both well-prepared. It's not just being a good host—it sets a tone of competence that reflects well on the facilitator. It builds a sense of goodwill and trust that extends into the meeting itself. Less agility on the facilitator's part will be required as a result.

You cannot build rapport with participants if you're still setting up chairs when they arrive.

One specific component of set-up is supplies. Be sure you've brought with you whatever materials you prefer to use, arrive in plenty of time to distribute them and keep them within easy reach. (You can find a printable copy of our Facilitation Supply List in the online toolkit.) You can then transition seamlessly to a new activity, planned or not, without having to rifle through your bag of supplies in order to switch gears. And bring lots. Participants should never have to be aware of you running out of handouts or markers that work.

LEARN FROM IT

Early warning system

Place is not just physical—it also encompasses the vibe in the room. Another element of place that is key to agile facilitation is to watch the room carefully once the session is underway. Paying attention to group dynamics is a foundational facilitation skill and one that extends well beyond the scope of this book. For our purposes, it is worth noting that you need to be on a "reconnaissance mission" throughout the session, watching for clues that you need to pivot or fine-tune.

Have you ever attended a presentation during which the speaker has lost the attention of the room and yet does not adjust the delivery to get it back? She just carries on speaking to her too-long slide deck. Have you noticed how difficult it is to pay any attention to what that speaker is trying to communicate in that moment, because you are distracted by how unaware she is? Again, you want to avoid being the Oblivious Facilitator.

Having an early warning system in place is particularly important if a conflict is brewing, or if you are losing the engagement of key players in a process. One of the most common fears I hear from new facilitators is the fear of not knowing how to handle a difficult participant. Here's the secret: don't give them an opportunity to become difficult in the first place! In coaching facilitators how to deal with problematic behaviour in a session, Michael Wilkinson[71] highlights the fact that only gentler interventions are needed when you employ early detection. The consequences of disengagement are lower when we catch it early, and it takes less active intervention to draw people back in. A meaningful glance or repositioning your body may be all it takes to encourage a participant to re-engage positively. If you notice. But if you have missed the cues that someone is on the verge of checking out of a process, you will need to work far harder to draw that person back in later on. By then the stakes are higher. More on this later, but the key takeaway at this stage is to monitor the room carefully throughout the session. As a facilitator, your responsibility is not just to select and equip an appropriate venue, but to act as the guardian of the atmosphere in that space.

Translators

The facilitator has a lot to do once a session has started. Also, the facilitator is often new to the group. As such, you may not appreciate the unstated dynamics of a conversation, you may be unfamiliar with the nuances, and you may miss certain details. It is therefore helpful to have informants in the room whose job it is to monitor what is happening and to translate those dynamics for the facilitator's benefit. A combination of external and internal helpers is ideal. Bring along a colleague, ideally someone also skilled enough in facilitation that she can pay attention alongside you. Internal translators can also be given the task of communicating subtleties that you are likely to have missed. Keep an eye on them throughout the session in case they are trying to get your attention. You can also check in with this team on breaks or during group activities to confirm things are on track.

I have used these translators to my advantage on multiple occasions, sometimes by design and often by serendipity, when they have been kind enough to alert me to what is going on. Sometimes their role is as simple as explaining an acronym. But in one recent case, I was informed at a break that one of the most vocal participants had actually been on leave for the past two months and had just come in to work for this particular session, such that many of her comments were outdated or irrelevant, unbeknownst to her or to me.

Multiple perspectives are always protective ...

... so it is a good idea to be deliberate in gathering them as the session unfolds.

Process

	In advance **ANTICIPATION**	In the room **AGILITY**	Afterwards **ABSORPTION**
PEOPLE	About you About others	About you About others	About you About others
PURPOSE	Clarify it Use it	Clarify it Use it	Clarify it Use it
PLACE	Leverage it Learn from it	Leverage it Learn from it	Leverage it Learn from it
PROCESS	Script it Hold it loosely	**Script it Hold it loosely**	Script it Hold it loosely

The burning question you've probably been holding onto throughout the entire book is what to do when the process you are facilitating isn't working as well as anticipated. We'll get there, I promise. But before we do, I want to reinforce the idea that there is a lot you can do in advance of the session to mitigate the need for nimble facilitation behaviour. If you have prepared thoroughly and anticipated accurately, your need for the agility skills I am about to describe will be significantly reduced. Do those things first.

One more reminder: it also helps to consider whose job it is to get a group back on track. The process design is the facilitator's responsibility, but the achievement of the objectives needs to stay with the group. It is common for a facilitator under pressure to assume more responsibility for the group's situation than she should. In turn, the group can be too willing to turn over its responsibility to the facilitator, when in fact it needs to rest with the team. The purpose was set by them and ultimately its achievement rests with them. The facilitator's job is to create a structure within which they can solve the problem at hand. This dance demonstrates why it is so important for the facilitator and the group to be well in sync with one another. They each have a role to play in ensuring the session's success.

Let me give you two examples to illustrate this point. There are times when participants' behaviour is distracting the group. Perhaps they are holding side conversations, checking their phones, or bringing up points that are tangential to the task at hand. That is a good time to remind the whole group that the outcomes were set by them and rest with them to achieve. A similar reminder is sometimes needed when a group is developing an implementation plan or a to-do list. If this exercise is happening at the end of a long session, it is common for the group to sit back and let the facilitator take responsibility for documenting next steps. Yet ironically, those next steps will likely not involve the facilitator at all. They belong with the group. This concept may sound obvious, but in the heat of the moment when a process does not appear to be working as well as you'd hoped, remember that the facilitator may need to step back rather than lean in.

We will consider how to manage effective process in the room through a case study of what not to do, and a tip sheet containing ideas to get you moving when a group is stuck.

SCRIPT IT

Your job is to help the group make progress toward the intended purpose, courtesy of a process you have designed in advance. That process is your script and it includes several options that will allow you to respond to the outcomes, timing and energy level in real time. You are tweaking it and/or making choices as things unfold.

Yet once in the room, progress can stall. It can be difficult to discern which option to choose or which pathway to follow. In this section, I offer tips to help get unstuck—whether it's the group or you that needs that help. Note that in this first section, it's largely irrelevant why the session is stuck. It's happened, you're in the moment, and it's your job to fix it. The important thing is to have a set of tools to get it back on track.

Getting unstuck

This tip sheet is supplied online as a printable resource in our Sage Solutions free resource library.[72] Keep it in your facilitation folder and whip it out in those moments when you're stuck. In this section I'll go into detail about each point and some specific actions you can try.

The group is stuck

Getting Unstuck

This is your Rescue Resource. Print it and bring it with you to every session. Think of it as your process first aid kit.

1. Make the objectives visible.
2. Adjust when needed.
3. Don't panic.
4. Take a break.
5. Highlight accomplishments
6. Diagnose the source of the problem.
7. Establish ground rules.
8. Keep the group onside.
9. Name the elephant.
10. Share the responsibility.
11. Clarify the instructions.
12. Switch to Plan B.
13. Swap learning styles.
14. Align activity with intent.
15. Use a 'generic exercise.'
16. Keep your sense of humour.
17. Do something unexpected.
18. Hang in there.

1. **Make the objectives visible.** Review the purpose of the session. Is this purpose visible to everyone? This includes any associated objectives. This is an important touchstone, for you and participants. Sometimes simply re-reading it aloud is enough to reorient the group in a more productive direction.

2. **Adjust when needed.** If things aren't working, don't pretend they are. If you are on the wrong train, staying on it longer won't help you get on the right track. Course correct as needed.

3. **Don't panic.** Stay present and as relaxed as possible, so that you can think. Remember your intention to stay curious. Resist the urge to make this about you. Maintain your attention outward, on the people and the purpose.

4. **Take a break.** Even if one wasn't scheduled, the group likely needs it and you do too. Preferably include movement and fresh air. For you and them. This may prove more challenging than it sounds, especially if people want to make suggestions and ask questions. Engage with them if you need to, but suggest you do it over a walk perhaps?

5. **Highlight accomplishments.** Summarizing progress accomplishes two things: it affirms productive progress, and it gives your brain additional time to process possible ways forward. Even better: invite someone in the group to do the recap.

6. **Diagnose the problem.** Why are things off the rails? Is it a process issue? A group dynamics/personality problem? Low energy level? The complexity of the problem at hand? Choose your next strategy to match the source of the difficulty.

7. **Establish ground rules.** Sometimes meetings go off the rails because people are failing to honour their commitments to each other and the process. Maybe someone is dominating the conversation while others are disengaging. Were the ground rules set clearly at the start? Do they need to be reinforced? It is the facilitator's job to be the guardian of respectful behaviour.

8. **Keep the group on side.** Are people feeling heard? Do the tasks you are giving them seem meaningful? Ensure that you are using their

words, giving them relevant assignments and involving them in the process. You don't want them stuck due to frustration with you.

9. **Name the elephant.** Make explicit to the group what you are noticing and what choices they have in response. This does three things: it makes explicit something the group might be struggling with; it helps people organize their [currently muddled] thinking; it reminds everyone that responsibility for the outcomes lies with the group.

10. **Share the responsibility.** Ask the group where to go next. It's usually best to invite several suggestions, or create a couple of scenarios and check which the group prefers. This approach shares the responsibility of achieving the purpose. Often someone else in the room can see a way through the fog when you can't. It is an asset to acknowledge your fallibility and to be what Amy Edmondson refer to as the "master of I don't know."[73]

11. **Clarify the instructions.** Tweak the activity. Sometimes people just need the task explained in a new way. Or to be given different constraints. Or more creative prompts from you, to help them adjust their perspective. Working through an example with them ("Let's do the first one together...") can really help.

12. **Switch to Plan B.** Dig into your toolbox of facilitation techniques— or at least refer to your notes. This is when your preparation comes in handy. When your brain is too full to be creative, you can rely on the thinking you did in advance. Switching to your Plan B or C is not a failure, it's a recognition that a new pathway needs to be tried.

13. **Swap learning styles.**[74] If you have been relying heavily on listening and logic, see if you can find ways to make the process more visual or intuitive. Often a group gets stuck because some people are talking too much, and others disengage. Consider reframing the task to be more active.

14. **Align activity with intent.** Maybe it's time, for instance, to move from discussion to decision. Certain activities are better suited to certain kinds of group activity; brainstorming is for generating ideas, while dot voting is intended to inform priority setting or decision

making. Misalignment between the activity and the intent can cause a group to spin its wheels. Align your choice of technique with what the group needs to accomplish at this time in the process.

15. **Use a generic exercise.** Having a 'generic but helpful' exercise at the ready is a great way to change up the focus. Ask people to write two suggestions on an index card, then you mix them up and read them aloud. Give each person a piece of coloured paper and ask them what they would do if they were in charge and had to make a decision based on what they know right now. Invite them to stand up and declare the best idea they've heard all day. Any of these activities could fit, no matter what is happening in the room at the time. They are helpful to have in your toolbox as they can move things forward, help you "take the temperature" of the room, and give you time to think.

16. **Keep your sense of humour.** Be lighthearted and reassuring. Maintaining your sense of humour, even as your heart rate is rising, is a powerful way to remain connected to your participants. Sometimes openly acknowledging when things are difficult is all it takes to reset the dynamic.

17. **Do something unexpected.** Introducing an element of surprise can shake people out of a rut. Maybe you pull out some candy. Ask people to switch seats while you put on some lively music. Play an improv game with the group. When in doubt, head outside!

18. **Hang in there.** Convince yourself to stick it out just a little bit longer. Sometimes things get messy right before a breakthrough. Be patient. Your patience for apparent detours should probably exceed the group's by at least a few minutes. Trust the group and your planning and wait it out.

You're stuck

It's great to know that we have the tools to get out of difficult situations, but what about building awareness for how to avoid them in the first place. What got us stuck? Let's look at situations where the derailment is caused by the facilitator. What's gone wrong? How does your behaviour need to change?

I recall a large session in which I was a participant (admittedly a challenge for me at the best of times, as I'm more comfortable running the meeting!). The facilitator asked the group of about 140 people how many were familiar with a particular facilitation methodology. Roughly 80% of the room raised their hands. Instead of adjusting his plan or his delivery based on that feedback, the facilitator carried on to confess that this technique was new to him (strike one), explained it tentatively and with little relevance to the task at hand (strike two), and led the group through it poorly (strike three). Let's unpack this example a bit more:

- **Strike one:** I am a fan of candour from the front of the room. But in this case, self-identifying as a rookie in a room of veterans undermined people's confidence in the facilitator and the process from the start. Drawing attention to the methodology itself instead of to its purpose further put the spotlight onto the facilitator, making the moment about him instead of about the group's needs.

- **Strike two:** When using any technique or activity, the instructions should be clear, as should the relevance of the task to the objectives at hand. In this case, vague instructions and skepticism as to the eventual usefulness of the feedback requested led to numerous questions that the facilitator was not equipped to answer. The room was full of buzz, but it was murmuring and grumbling, not the excited kind.

- **Strike three:** As the activity unfolded, people increasingly lost their way. When a task did not work well, the group was asked to move on to step two rather than clarifying or improving step one. Some participants complied without any investment in the outcome, while others disengaged and still others became overtly frustrated. Things were definitely off the rails.

Ideally, you won't let your behaviour be the reason you need to pull things back on track. But if you fear you are derailing the group, my first suggestion is to remind yourself of the 18 tips above. Many of them work just as well for getting the facilitator back on the rails as they do for the group. Also, trust your preparation and go back to it. All the way back, to the part about knowing yourself. What do you most need right now to be effective? Create space for that.

Specifically, what might that look like? Maybe like this:

- Give the group a task and escape to the bathroom to breathe.

- Invite participants to co-create a way forward. "At this point we could do xyz or abc. Which approach seems most helpful right now?"

- Slow things way down. Recap, or allow a bit of silence. Chances are, you are in more of a rush than they are.

- Complete the following sentence, and/or invite participants to do so: "If we are here to achieve _____, and we've so far established that _____, then our next helpful step is _____."

- Invite the group to join you in "clearing your head"—maybe by going outside or adding in some movement, but with an explicit objective of resetting.

- Might it be time to be done for the day? Things always seem clearer in the morning!

HOLD IT LOOSELY

While the above section was primarily about keeping things on the rails, this section focuses on addressing head-on some common occurrences that threaten to cause a derailment. These are challenges that are initially outside your control, so you may need to be more flexible in your response to them. It's like catching a baseball; if your arm and wrist are stiff, the ball smacks your palm and bounces out of the glove. Keep a soft hand.

Dealing with challenging people

In my training sessions, facilitation students' biggest concern is dealing with difficult participants. Those people who seem certain to force you away from your script. Handling disruptive folks therefore warrants its own section here to ease your fear. Sometimes their behaviour takes the form of aggression ("the hijacker") while at other times it is expressed as withdrawal from the process ("the deserter"). Here are several ways to address both:

- First, remember that the fear of difficult behaviour is more common than the difficult behaviour itself. If you do your job well, the likelihood of people behaving badly is lower than you might think.[75]

- Good process prevents bad behaviour. If people are engaged in meaningful, purposeful activities and are feeling heard, they rarely have a need to "misbehave" in a group. Similarly, if they know they will be given three breaks in a day to check their messages, they are less likely to check their phones at inappropriate times. Prevention is the best medicine.

- Don't jump to conclusions. A sour-faced participant may be quite content, but processing tricky content. Conversely, a smile might contain more sarcasm than support. Be careful not to make assumptions about what you are seeing. Test them out.[76]

- Don't ignore disruptive behaviours, at least not for long. They almost inevitably grow. (Like needing to pee in the middle of the night!) As other people notice both the behaviour and your unwillingness to address it, they too tend to lose trust and disengage.

- Check in to make sure that the behaviour really is problematic. It may be very short-lived, or necessary, or less of a problem to the group than to you. For example, if you are working cross-culturally, you may interpret a pattern of behaviour as aggressive while locally it would simply be seen as animated and engaged.

- Recognize whose responsibility it is. If the behaviour involves one individual, you may not want to enlist the whole group to address it. Or, it may have nothing to do with you or the process at hand and therefore not be yours to address at all.

- Insist on respectful behaviour in the room. If the group has developed ground rules, it is your responsibility to enforce them. If they haven't, perhaps now is the time. Most people share a sense of what reasonable behavioural expectations are.

- Ask questions rather than being prescriptive. Offer choices. For example, "I am noticing that a number of you are on your phones, yet we have not quite finished the task at hand. Do we need to take a break now, or would you prefer to push through, giving this your full attention for 15 more minutes to get it done before we take our scheduled break?"

- Intervene early and in small ways before the stakes get higher. There are usually clues that precede people getting really upset, such as gradual changes in body language or tone of voice. Watch for those and make slight adjustments before behaviour becomes highly problematic and your interventions in response need to be more extreme.

- Address the problem cleanly and with candour.[77] Naming what you are seeing or feeling can make it safer for the group to do the same. Try something along the lines of "Wow, that was an intense contribution! It made me feel a sense of heaviness. Is anyone else sensing something similar? What needs to happen before we can continue?"

- Democratize the process. Select a technique that invites every person in the room to contribute and to become aware of each other's contributions, such as writing ideas on three sticky notes and posting them visually on the wall, or doing a round-robin activity in which each person speaks. This encourages the quieter participants to engage and the more dominant personalities to equalize their input with everyone else's.

- Assess whether dissenting opinions are outliers or widely held. If you have someone insisting on the group's behalf that "everyone knows xyz…" or "it's obvious that abc is true…," you can initiate an [anonymous] activity to test the accuracy of these statements. For example, invite people to write their opinion on a piece of paper and put it in a bowl on their way out the door on a break. You can then read the answers during the break and report the findings back to the group as a whole. Or, create a spectrum on the wall that shows the range of opinion on the subject at hand. Invite participants to write an X on the spectrum in the position that reflects their opinion. Once everyone has added their X to the page, the whole group (including the domineering personality who started all of this) can see how opinions are clustered within the room. It provides some evidence to counteract or affirm the assumptions being voiced.

Unexpected news

Sometimes the bombshell in the room is not related to disruptive behaviour as much as to disruptive content, perhaps shared for the first time in the session. Although rare (thankfully), this scenario does require some extra process agility in the room.

Let me paint a few scenarios for you. Perhaps the meeting sponsor decides to announce an upcoming round of layoffs during the meeting. Or perhaps she lets something slip that makes the group wonder if a leadership change is imminent, but then is not at liberty to say any more. Another possibility might involve a participant being triggered by something in the session, resulting in tears and/or a dramatic exit. Or maybe a key player is absent from the session, and it then becomes known that he was let go the day before. Or it could be that someone decides to disclose a serious health scare or a decision to leave the company.

I had it happen where a key player in a project had been let go on a Friday afternoon. Our facilitated meeting that we'd been planning for months was scheduled for early the following week. It was an invited, but not closed session—that is, we let specific people/groups know about it, but in theory anyone was welcome to attend. This former employee showed up at the meeting, ostensibly as a member of the public. He'd been a well-known municipal employee who was key to this project, so having him sit in the gallery throughout was awkward and unexpected, even more so because most people would not have yet heard about his dismissal. This story highlights the need to be ready for anything and to arrive early enough to handle unexpected turns of events. Luckily, I had spoken to him upon his arrival to find out what level of participation he expected to have and to manage how best to handle that.

Whatever the specifics, the scenario leaves everyone with their mouths hanging open, gasping. As the facilitator, what do you do?

The Oblivious Facilitator would simply carry on with this script as if nothing had happened. Don't be that person.

By now, I hope my suggested responses are becoming obvious: give yourself and the group a moment to catch your breath. Let the news land. Take a few breaths. Then, acknowledge the "bigness" of that news. Perhaps explore some feelings that it might be eliciting ("I can imagine you are feeling gobsmacked right now..."). Then ask the sponsor or the group what they would most like to do next. Options could range from taking a break, to addressing the big issue that has just been raised, to carrying on with the original agenda. Depending on the sensitivities involved, that decision might need to be made offline, so a break might be essential either way so that you and your client can sort out next steps. You may also need gently to remind people of some "rules of engagement" during the break—including using the room more than the corridors to address issues of relevance to the whole group, for example, or maintaining confidentiality about what is going on (i.e. staying off their phones).

An unexpected behaviour or sudden shock to the group doesn't have to make you drop your whole plan. If you're holding your script loosely, and have the tools prepared to make adjustments, then you can weather the most surprising of challenges.

Afterwards: Absorption

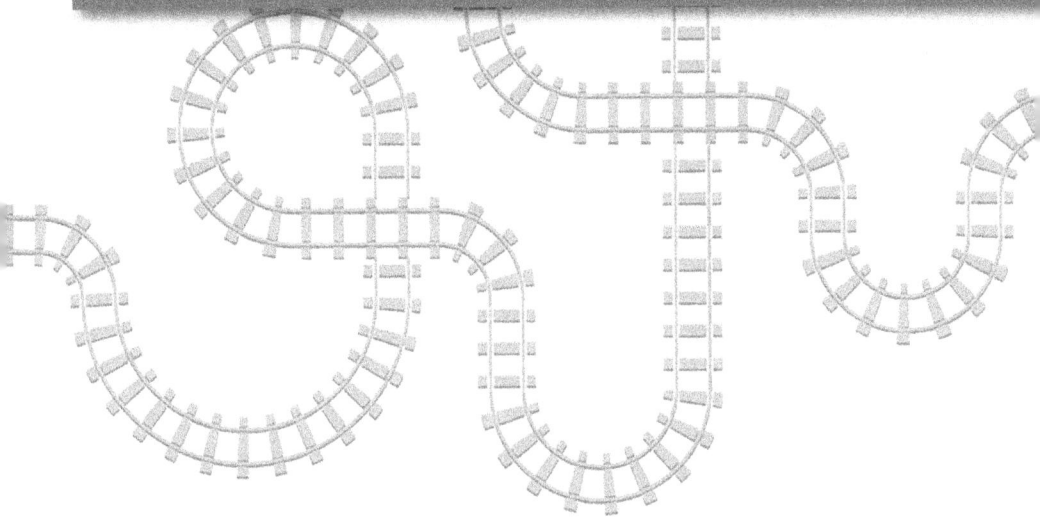

And then it's over. Whew! You did it. It's a bit like finishing a day at an amusement park—you're likely experiencing a huge adrenaline rush followed by a crash of exhaustion. I trust you're proud of yourself for being brave, and you have a sense you'll be even braver next time. You may even want to try that roller coaster one more time, but you know it's time to wrap things up. Almost.

It might seem that once a meeting is finished, whether it's gone off the rails or not, your job as a nimble facilitator is done. Not so, if you want to further hone your craft.

Each new facilitation experience provides an opportunity to learn and improve. The event happens in the room, but the learning happens afterwards, and only so far as you are intentional about ensuring it. In this section, we will explore ways to translate your experience into continuous learning.

Afterwards is also the best time to reconnect with your client, not only to debrief but also to pave the way for future collaboration. Discipline and imagination are both required, at a time when you might be tempted to collapse into a weary heap. When we are tired, we need to rely on systems and habits we've established in advance for following up and finishing well. This final section of the book will coach you through doing so.

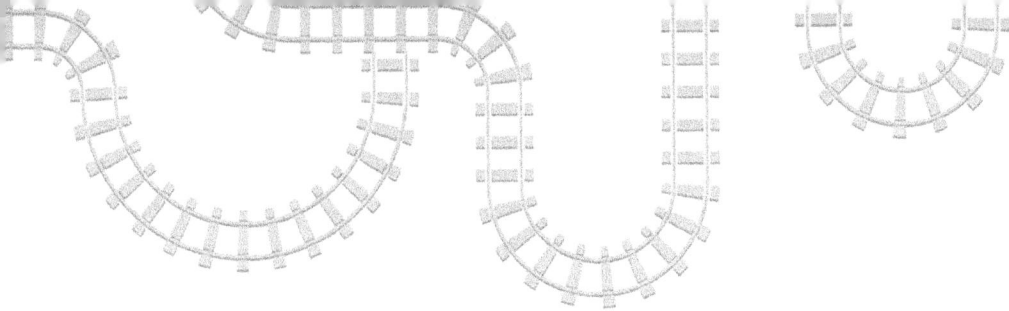

People

	In advance **ANTICIPATION**	In the room **AGILITY**	Afterwards **ABSORPTION**
PEOPLE	About you About others	About you About others	**About you** **About others**
PURPOSE	Clarify it Use it	Clarify it Use it	Clarify it Use it
PLACE	Leverage it Learn from it	Leverage it Learn from it	Leverage it Learn from it
PROCESS	Script it Hold it loosely	Script it Hold it loosely	Script it Hold it loosely

The session is done and you fear it went badly. In fact, you're sure it did. Or perhaps you think it might just have gone brilliantly. How do you know? Again we'll look at both yourself and others in making our assessments.

ABOUT YOU

Let's start with you. Did you do a good job? Did you leave your client keen to book you again in the future?

Perspective

First, who gets to decide how a session went? Are you basing your judgement only on your own assessment? If so, beware. As facilitators, our perspective on how things went can be very different from the perspective of others in the room. We are highly invested in the details of the process. We likely pay it far closer attention than anyone else does. Remember that others did not see our script in advance. Our intentions of how the process was going to go aren't known to the group, and frankly, are rarely relevant to them, especially afterwards. Beating ourselves up about or apologizing for something hypothetical that did not happen is completely unnecessary. Similarly, assuming something went very well simply because it followed *our* expectations can also miss the mark.

Self compassion

This question of perspective brings us full circle, to the ways in which your self-knowledge equips you for your facilitation role. If you recognize a tendency to be hard on yourself, then it is quite possible that the meeting did not go as badly as your inner critic (what my colleague Nancy Watt[78] calls your "headitor") is telling you it did. What evidence do you have that leads you to the conclusions you are drawing? Are you giving more mental airtime to negative feedback than to positive? Pay attention to the story you're telling yourself before you head into a more systematic debrief with the various audiences outlined below. Drawing on Kristin Neff's work, Brené Brown expresses it this way: talk to yourself the way you'd talk to someone you love.[79] First, affirm what went really well and learn from that.

Remember too that in advance, we use our anticipation skills to design a script based on our best guess. If things unfold differently in real life than expected, perhaps we could not realistically have predicted them any more accurately than we did, short of being clairvoyant. If you did diligent preparation and used your full toolkit of skills and positive behaviours in the room, it is likely that the session went as well as it reasonably could have been expected to go.

And perhaps it went even better than that. You know what decisions you made and what trade-offs you considered as the process occurred in real time. Had you decided differently, or been less nimble and intentional throughout, things could have landed in a much more problematic place. There's no telling how far off the rails the session might have gone in the absence of your skilled facilitation!

ABOUT OTHERS

It is also worth noting that we all have a tendency to see our view as true rather than as one subjective interpretation of a shared experience. Brené Brown refers to these as "confabulations; lies that are honestly told and treated as fact rather than opinion."[80] As Peter McIntyre writes, "Confidence comes not from always being right, but from not fearing to be wrong." We need to be willing to be wrong even about how the session when, by tempering our own perspectives with consideration of how others thought the session went. This is about holding even your own beliefs nimbly! That's a hard thing to do. Failing to have this kind of open-mindedness about being wrong is a significant block to our own learning.

Client/Sponsor

One primary line of accountability is to your client or sponsor of the meeting. What did that person think of how the session went? It is important to assess from the client's perspective how well you achieved the results for which you were selected for this task.[81] Consider how and when you will find out their perspective. Be both courageous and thorough in this conversation. Go beyond, "So, how do you think things went?" to ask more pointed questions that will be more likely to help you improve. How would the conversation deepen, for example, if you were to ask something like, "Can you offer a couple of specific ways I could have handled things more effectively in the session?" or "Are there any follow-up steps I can take now that would help to improve the lasting positive results of our time together?" This debrief is also useful for maintaining a productive, ongoing connection with this person as a trusted advisor. It provides you with an opportunity to thank, encourage and/or impress her, so use it well.

Participants

Next, consider if/how you will connect with the other participants to learn from their perspectives. My first tip is to move beyond distributing a quick, generic evaluation page as they rush out the door, for two reasons. People are unlikely to give you thoughtful feedback when they are done for the day. They are tired and have mentally moved on. And the questions on such forms are rarely specific enough to give you feedback you can immediately and concretely apply. I therefore recommend a few fixes:

- If you decide to use an evaluation form on-site, leave time for it. Sometimes I even ask participants to fill it in during the second-to-last time slot of the day so they are willing to give it their full attention.

- On that form, use detailed questions with deliberate wording. For example, consider the differences in likely responses between a question such as, "How relevant was the content of today's workshop?" compared to, "What is one specific skill you learned today that you are likely to apply within the next two weeks?"

- Consider distributing a feedback survey electronically within 48 hours of the session. There are trade-offs to adopting this approach. You may get fewer responses, and respondents may have mentally shifted back to their daily grind and be less tuned in to the specifics of the workshop than they were at the time. But those who do respond may do so more thoughtfully and with the benefit of some perspective not accessible to them in the room.

- A "mixed methodology" may be preferable, where you ask for people's top-of-mind feedback as they leave the room, using a method intentionally designed to be quick and visual such as putting a series of sticker dots on an evaluation continuum. Then afterwards, you send participants a couple of more thought-provoking, detailed application questions that will both help you to improve and further their own learning too.

- Remember to keep the scale of the feedback expectation aligned with the scope of the session itself. A complex feedback mechanism is overkill for a two-hour, one-off session but might be entirely appropriate for a multi-day summit to inform the work of an ongoing team.

- You can also intentionally ask participants for their feedback on how to make the session better during the session itself, either from the front of the room or informally on breaks. Asking, then acting on, their input builds their trust and allegiance. It also gives you the opportunity to improve the session in real time rather than afterwards when it is too late for that cohort to benefit from what you are hearing.

In some cases, it is appropriate for you to follow up personally with participants afterwards, particularly if you have an ongoing relationship with them. Individually, they will offer a different perspective on the meeting, and you can use this additional touch point to improve your practice, to reinforce their learnings from the session and to strengthen your connection with them. You never know when you might have the opportunity to work with them again.

At the same time, beware of the "jury of one," whether that one is you or someone else. A single perspective is just that—one person's point of view. In my own practice, I find it challenging not to focus on the one most negative comment in a stack of evaluation forms. I once fixated on a participant's feedback that the facilitation pace was far too fast. I do speak and move quickly through the world, so this is feedback I have received since I was young. I found myself ruminating on how I could have slowed things down while still honouring the time frames and objectives I had been given from the client, completely ignoring the several other comments about how much participants had enjoyed the high energy level and productivity of the day. I subsequently learned that the one negative comment came from someone who was recovering from surgery and was on medication that made her sleepy. No wonder the session seemed to be unfolding too quickly! We have a tendency to give certain voices more space in our heads, so be sure to elicit as many opinions as you can. Remember, multiple perspectives are protective.

It is also worth paying attention to your favourite feedback trap, so you can avoid it. Perhaps you tend to reject the feedback you receive, instead becoming defensive and entrenched. Or maybe you take on all feedback, behaving as if anyone's perspective has more value than your own. Or worse, you might use feedback as a tool to bludgeon yourself about your own insecurities, making it mean more than it does until you're a complete mess that will never facilitate again! Try to hold the feedback at enough distance to find the usefulness in it without triggering your own defence mechanisms. There is always something to learn, even from opinions with which we disagree. As Aristotle noted, "It is the mark of an educated mind to be able to entertain a thought without accepting it."

Purpose

	In advance **ANTICIPATION**	In the room **AGILITY**	Afterwards **ABSORPTION**
PEOPLE	About you About others	About you About others	About you About others
PURPOSE	Clarify it Use it	Clarify it Use it	**Clarify it Use it**
PLACE	Leverage it Learn from it	Leverage it Learn from it	Leverage it Learn from it
PROCESS	Script it Hold it loosely	Script it Hold it loosely	Script it Hold it loosely

In addition to seeking out multiple perspectives, it is worth considering the standards against which we will gauge the success of a session. The achievement of the purpose is your primary gauge for how things went.

CLARIFY IT

This is the opportunity to go back to your original, co-created objectives and assess how thoroughly they were achieved. Remember that every session will have objectives related to both content and experience. Assess its success accordingly.

Content

To what extent did the group achieve its original content-related outcomes? Did those outcomes shift at all during the session, and if so, were those new purposes fulfilled? Was additional substantive progress made that extended beyond the expressed objectives? How was all of this progress documented?

Be systematic here. Completing this exercise is helpful for several reasons. Often it will encourage you, by objectively demonstrating that more was accomplished in the session than you perhaps thought at the time. It can also be used to capture or reinforce the success of the session to your client. Finally, it will reveal gaps or opportunities that can guide your next steps.

Experience

What about experiential aims: did relationships grow or deteriorate, for example, as a result of participating in the session? Did participants enjoy themselves? Was learning evident? If participants came out of your session with a buzz, that enthusiasm is going to have a significant impact on their chances of retaining your key message.

By capturing the extent to which both kinds of objectives were achieved, you generate a more complete picture of the usefulness of the session.

USE IT

An additional element of a session's larger purpose, from your perspective as the facilitator, is to improve your skills. This learning happens through experience, but is accelerated when you are deliberate about becoming a more reflective practitioner. Instead of aiming to run a perfect session, your aim should be to facilitate a session that improves all your future sessions. Ironically, this lack of perfectionism is likely to lead to a better session!

Choose to learn

We've heard that "experience is the greatest teacher." But learning from experience is not automatic. It is quite possible to experience things without learning from them, and the premise of this book is that it is also possible to learn without direct experience, but rather through the experience of others. Ideally, the two would go hand in hand. The first step is to be purposeful about choosing to adopt the stance of a learner, especially when faced with sessions that went differently than expected.

Teachability is an incredibly valuable skill. It is one my daughters have learned through competitive dance and are now applying to other areas of their lives. I have heard one of them repeat the mantra of one of their instructors—"corrections are gold"—when giving feedback to members of teams she leads. This attitude is key to being an effective and nimble facilitator. As the George Santayana quote made famous by Winston Churchill goes, "Those who cannot remember the past are condemned to repeat it."

This stance of teachability is further reinforced by recent work in the field of "failing forward." For example, John Maxwell argues that the perception and fear of failure is often paralyzing, preventing us from being creative and making important mistakes.[82] When we accept that failure is a natural and necessary part of the process, we can shift into failure as an opportunity for learning and move forward with confidence. Amy Edmondson states, "I'm not pro-failure, I'm pro-learning," emphasizing the value of failure to accelerate learning.[83]

Choose which lessons

Just as learning from experience is not automatic, neither is it self-evident what life lessons a learning experience will yield. Even when you do intentionally want to learn from your experience, there are multiple possible lessons to be learned, and you can choose what you will draw from that experience.[84] For example, if a friend recounts an experience of getting a speeding ticket and says, "I learned my lesson," it begs the question of what he learned. Not to speed? Not to get caught? To negotiate more effectively with the police officer for a lower fine? Similarly, if a facilitated session goes differently than expected, the lessons you can learn from that variance are not automatic. Your takeaway may be that your time management skills need improvement. Or that next time you will work to define the purpose more clearly in advance. Or that it is virtually impossible to predict accurately what humans will do. Or perhaps your conclusion will be never to work with that client again!

I'm part of a professional development group called Thought Leaders Business School, and our tribe has created an effective culture around intentional learning. Members are encouraged to share with candour and vulnerability not only what happened to them, but also what learnings they took from it. You might hear "I did this speaking gig recently where I used a real-time surveying software tool to get the audience to participate in the presentation. This allowed me to learn a lot about the kind of people in the room, so my presentation was much more effective." Equally, a story might be shared about misjudging the audience, and how the speaker intends to prepare better next time.

The link between experience and learning is reflexivity, which is reflection plus change. Our goal in becoming a nimble facilitator is to become a reflexive practitioner—to reflect on our experience and to apply what we have learned. Donald Schon wrote about reflective practice in the 1980s, building on 1910 work by Dewey.[85] Working in the field of education, he highlighted the importance of "reflection-on-action"—thinking more deeply about how a class went, the options available to you at the time, why you chose as you did and what you hope to choose next time. Intentionality is key here, as reflective practice "allows distress to inform a redirection to new landmarks without being overwhelmed, or blinded by the familiar."[86] Be deliberate in your work after the session to capture what you have learned.

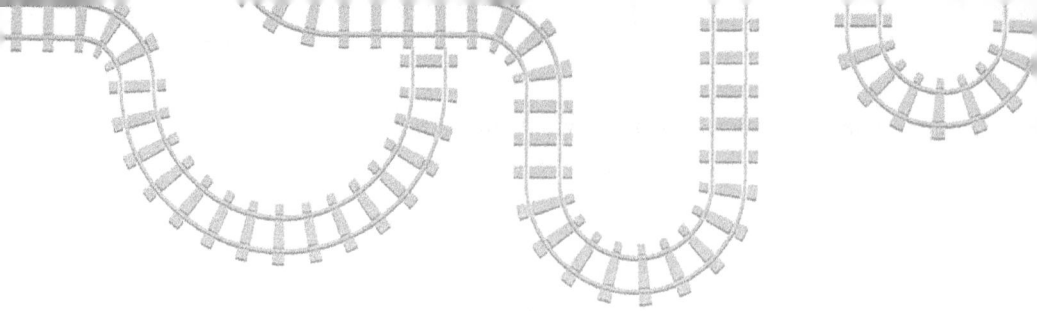

Place

	In advance ANTICIPATION	In the room AGILITY	Afterwards ABSORPTION
PEOPLE	About you About others	About you About others	About you About others
PURPOSE	Clarify it Use it	Clarify it Use it	Clarify it Use it
PLACE	Leverage it Learn from it	Leverage it Learn from it	**Leverage it Learn from it**
PROCESS	Script it Hold it loosely	Script it Hold it loosely	Script it Hold it loosely

Admittedly, most of the facilitation nimbleness work related to place—both in terms of venue selection and the vibe in the room—happens before and during the session the session rather than afterwards. There are, however, a few practical tips related to ending well that help to differentiate good from great when it comes to nimble facilitation. And of course, there's a lot we can learn from the different places we've chosen to host our sessions.

LEVERAGE IT

It's over when the last participant leaves

People remember endings.[87] It is therefore critical as a nimble facilitator that you leverage that knowledge to ensure you end a session well. Just as you create the tone at the start of a session, you are also responsible for shaping and maintaining that tone until the last participant leaves. Behave as a hospitable host would, upon both arrival and departure. This means resisting the urge to pack up your materials or check your phone or collapse exhausted into a chair until you have bid farewell to all participants. Reserve some energy for this. Be available to participants and most notably to the sponsor for a while after the session. Not only will people leave with a positive final impression of you, but you never know what questions you can answer or business development opportunities you can leverage during those final moments. More than a few of my contracts have emerged from conversations with participants who have attended previous sessions.

Not there and then

The best time to assess and learn from your performance is *not* at 4:30 p.m. on the final day of a session while still at the venue tidying up.

Need I say more? Right at the end of the session when you're tired is not a good time to decide how things went. You need the discipline to do so at a later point. Rest first. Get some air, some food and a change of scenery. Recharge before reflecting. You have entered the recuperation phase after the big race. You want to learn from your performance, but not until you've rehydrated and caught your breath. Facilitation takes a great deal of energy when things go as expected–even more so when they don't. Resist the urge to draw any conclusions about the session until after you've refuelled and refreshed your perspective.

LEARN FROM IT

Two additional quick tips about learning from both the venue and the vibe:

Physical features of the space

Were there features of the venue that proved to be especially helpful or unexpectedly annoying? Was it too cold? Were the staff unfriendly? Did a participant get locked out by mistake? Is there a pillar in exactly the wrong spot that blocks clear sight lines to the screen? Take note of those in case you would ever like to rebook—or to remember not to. Add them to your Space Planning Checklist for next time. You think you'll remember forever, but you won't. Write it down. I keep a log now of good venues. This is not only for my own purposes—it's also useful if clients ask for venue suggestions, and they often do.

Group dynamics in the space

Based on the feedback you have now received from your sponsor and other participants, were there clues you saw in the room but ignored at your peril? Take note of those too. This is the time to check your own perceptions against what people are telling you. Was the guy you thought looked cranky actually thoroughly enjoying the session and simply working hard to assimilate new knowledge? Were there times when you thought you were moving too quickly, but then you heard that people appreciated the energetic pace? Was the person you thought was just quiet actually really looking for an opportunity to participate that she was not effectively offered?

I once led a session in which one of the most outgoing participants ranked one section poorly because she felt excluded and inhibited from participating. This surprised me, as she was smiling and vocal throughout the day. When I checked in with her afterwards, she indicated that she was really hoping to be chosen as a volunteer for one of the role plays and felt left out of the fun when she was not. Yet I had intentionally chosen other people, as a way of engaging them more. This example reminded me that what I see may not match what is happening internally for participants, so it is worth checking that alignment. In another case, I have let a quiet person stay quiet, not wanting to single him out, only to learn later that he felt ignored or even at times silenced by others at his table.

Facilitation is rife with judgement calls. Only afterwards can you learn whether you made good ones. By doing so, you are strengthening your instincts as a nimble facilitator. The better you can get at reading subtleties and at reinforcing your "spidey sense" in the room, the more effective you will be.

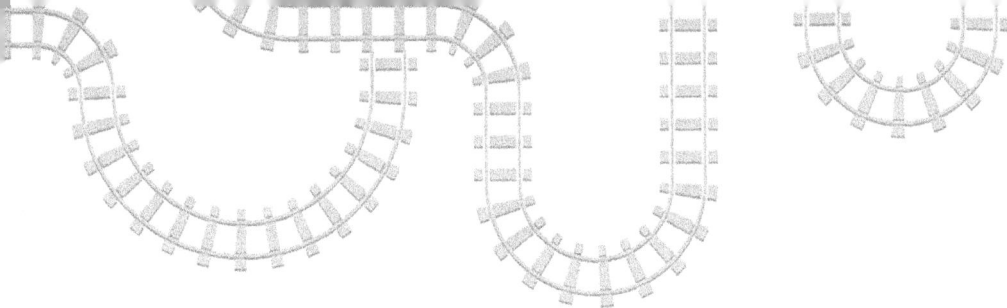

Process

	In advance ANTICIPATION	In the room AGILITY	Afterwards ABSORPTION
PEOPLE	About you About others	About you About others	About you About others
PURPOSE	Clarify it Use it	Clarify it Use it	Clarify it Use it
PLACE	Leverage it Learn from it	Leverage it Learn from it	**Leverage it Learn from it**
PROCESS	Script it Hold it loosely	Script it Hold it loosely	Script it Hold it loosely

When a session wraps up, it would be easy to discard your script. But don't be too hasty to do so. There is still time to strengthen it and even to grasp it less tightly, now from the perspective of a reflexive and nimble practitioner.

SCRIPT IT

Script your ending

We have already highlighted the importance of a strong ending. One way to ensure you remember to finish strongly is to design your ending intentionally and to include it in your facilitation script. Obviously, a lot of the work for scripting your ending has happened before your facilitation session began. But there's more to an ending than just the content that you've written out. It's about being both deliberate and responsive in the room, to ensure you follow through on your intention to finish well. Here are three practical tips for doing so:

1. **Leave time to end well.** Do not rush it. I am so committed to this idea that I frequently leave the final segment of my facilitation design intentionally blank. This is a balancing act, as we need our endings to be compelling enough to ensure participants stay with us. People leaving early is a surefire way to sap a group's energy. But we also need those same endings to leave some breathing space so that we don't arrive panting at the collective finish line. And realistically, if we've left a bit too much time even after a thoughtful ending, no one ever complains about a meeting that ends early!

2. **Recap and reframe.** Use the final minutes to clarify with the group what was accomplished. Doing so is a powerful way to bring things back on track if they risked losing focus at the end. That final wrap-up is also an opportunity to flag where many things may have stayed well on track and the few things that may have strayed toward a less desirable route. Or maybe toward an even better one.

3. **Help the group develop a clear to-do list.** Shared, explicit action steps with names and deadlines attached feel empowering because they affirm forward motion and time well spent. One additional insider tip on developing lists of action steps: include a column headed "What Done Looks Like." Use it to co-create with the group a shared understanding of what each key follow-up task involves, and how the group will know when it is complete. You'll be amazed at what assumptions this one exercise can surface—it is extremely helpful to ensure everyone has a similar understanding of the finish line for each task. Turn anticipated into actual.

Now that the session is over, your design initially based on anticipation turns into a record of what actually happened. After a session is an excellent time to compare the two, now with the wisdom of hindsight. As a reflexive practitioner, what are some concrete but not onerous ways we can be sure to learn from our almost-off-the-rails facilitation experiences? Here are a few possibilities:

- Be systematic and disciplined about your personal reflection. Some people like to maintain a professional journal, for example, where they note what they tried, how it went, what they wish they had done instead, and what they learned from the experience.

- You likely keep your facilitation designs on file. Go one step further by tracking two versions of that document: what you planned and what actually happened, including notes on what you learned and what you wish you'd done differently. Noting the differences between the two facilitation designs will be one of the most useful learning pieces you can do. By comparing them, you can get a sense of accurate your predictions are for a sessions, and how much your planning process may need to adapt in the future.

- Debrief with a colleague or coach. At times you may have a trusted colleague or co-facilitator in the room with whom to have a learning conversation. Or perhaps you have a skilled colleague who was not present but who is willing to be a sounding board for you afterwards. You may also choose to invest in the services of a more formal coach who is hired to help you level up in your facilitation practice. I have taken advantage of this type of service, and now offer it myself. Whatever the specifics may be, this conversation with a neutral and supportive third party is another way to absorb and gain perspective on what you have learned from your nimble facilitation experience.

- Look at the details of your specific recent design, but also at any fundamental facilitation skills that might need shoring up. For instance, I recently facilitated a session that came close to heading off the rails simply because I forgot to double check the size and amount of open wall space in the room. I arrived to find a packed space with no clear sight lines to spaces on the walls on which to hang flip chart paper. A rookie mistake. Fortunately, we were able to move the session to a larger space next door. But the close call was a good reminder to me not to neglect the basics.

You are never too experienced to go back to basics; use your delivery sessions as opportunities to refine the fundamentals.

HOLD IT LOOSELY

You still have an opportunity to hold your script, now informed by actual experience, lightly. Loosen your grip on it in at least two ways:

Treat it as practice for next time

Each facilitation experience is an opportunity to hone your craft. Just as you can't be rigid in your preparation or delivery, you should also stay loose when it comes to your follow up. Remember that you have now learned things from your most recent session that you could never have worked out just by thinking really hard about it. As Henry Ford famously said, "The only real mistake is the one from which we learn nothing."

It's not unlike science. Scientific experiments are designed to fail a lot of the time. We learn what works by learning what doesn't work. Scientists are used to considering unexpected results as learning opportunities rather than as failures. My experience has been similar in writing this book. It is important to me that it be a solid piece of work, but I also recognize that it is likely not the last—nor even the best—thing I will ever write. Maintaining that mindset allows me to give it my best without putting unnecessary or unhelpful pressure on myself. Facilitation is one context where paying attention to detail while resisting perfectionism is an important balancing act to master.

Teach it

Teaching something is a proven way to deepen your mastery of that subject, yet it may seem counterintuitive to suggest that teaching something is also a way to loosen your grip on it. Perhaps you fall into the category of folks who over-prepare and who only feel ready to lead a class once you've read everything ever written on the subject.

My experience has been the opposite of that. I have learned, through my years of teaching various subjects at several post-secondary institutions and privately in my practice, that teaching something reminds me that what I happened to do in the room is just one way it could have been done. Other skilled, creative people across time and around the world, and even in my own classroom, have successfully accomplished similar aims using other effective processes. Teaching helps me remember my place in my profession and perhaps to take myself a bit less seriously.

This principle reminds me of my cousin. She is a teacher who struggled with math as a student. Based on that experience, she now challenges herself to teach each new math concept in at least three different ways to her students. She recognizes that no single way will communicate effectively to everyone in the room. I can only assume that her self-imposed discipline of finding three ways to teach a concept helps her to maintain some flexibility around any one way of doing something. There is always another route to be found to arrive at the same destination.

Most of us move on too quickly from one facilitation assignment to the next thing on our to-do list, without taking time for systematic reflection and often with too much credence given to the overly critical voice in our head. By incorporating the steps suggested here, your toolbox and ability to recognize which tool to use are inevitably going to be much deeper the next time around.

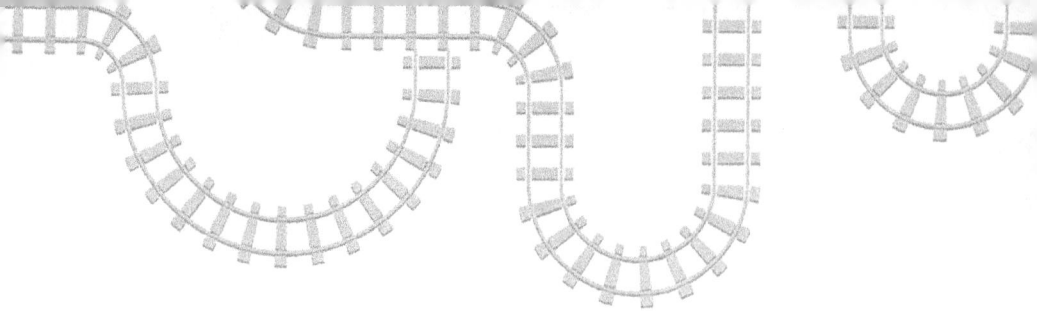

Wrapping up

As Yuval Noah Harari notes, "How do you live in a world where profound uncertainty is not a bug but a feature? To survive and flourish in such a world, you will need a lot of mental flexibility and great reserves of emotional balance. You will have to repeatedly let go of some of what you know best, and learn to feel at home with the unknown."[88]

A nimble facilitator is one who is equipped to let go of some of what he knows best and respond effectively to whatever happens in the moment. That is the point of all of this—the preparation, the awareness, the communication, the learning—it's all to give yourself a set of tools and some muscle memory to use in any scenario. That scenario might be a crazy one (did I tell you about the time a participant began circulating to each table in the room, telling people not to follow my instructions?) but it might also be oddly familiar as it follows almost exactly the scene you imagined in advance. The more experience you gain, the more you will find that the latter becomes the norm. Your anticipation skills become increasingly accurate. And if the opposite happens, where because of a context of volatility and complexity—and just the messiness of real life—your great process still leads to bad outcomes, stay curious about that. As Amy Edmondson writes, "The lack of simple cause-effect relationships in uncertain, ambiguous environments reinforces the importance of productive responses to outcomes of all kinds, but especially to bad news outcomes." [89] You'll be OK.

The point is not to anticipate everything with 100% accuracy. Nor is it to be flawless in front of the room. It's to be able to react nimbly to whatever happens in the moment, while maintaining your focus on the purpose.

And in regards to your participants, it's been said that you should make each session "a call to adventure your audience can't wait to take."[90] Consider what adventure you are calling them to, and embrace the adventure that you're on as well.

Like any adventure, this work takes considerable courage. Courage to accept that you can't control everything, but going out there anyway. Courage to walk into that session that feels daunting, relying on your preparation to see you through. Courage to trust that you are good enough. Courage to be authentic and therefore vulnerable in front of a room full of people. Courage to act not in the absence of fear, but despite it.

Brené Brown defines vulnerability as the courage to show up when you can't control the outcome. Is that not the definition of masterful facilitation? She writes that you can't engineer the uncertainty or discomfort out of vulnerability. Even by following all of the tips in this book, you will still often feel uncertain. Embrace that adrenaline rush—it's what makes facilitation exciting. And what makes you human. Ultimately, learning to be nimble is about learning to be a braver version of yourself. Learning is so uncomfortable. And so worth it. So be gentle with yourself, stay alert, and get a good night's sleep!

Endnotes

1   Brené Brown, *Dare to Lead: Brave Work. Tough Conversations. Whole Hearts* (New York: Random House, 2018): 20.

2   Chris Anderson, *TED Talks: The Official TED Guide to Public Speaking* (New York: Harper Collins, 2016).

3   D.C. Girasek, "How members of the public interpret the word accident," Injury Prevention 5 (1999): 19-25, http://dx.doi.org/10.1136/ip.5.1.19.

4   Donna McGeorge, 25 Minute Meeting (Milton: John Wiley & Sons Australia Ltd., 2018): 72.

5   Piers Ibbotson, *The Illusion of Leadership: Directing Creativity in Business and the Arts* (New York: Palgrave Macmillan, 2008): 3.

6   Charles Duhigg, *Smarter Faster Better: The Secrets of Being Productive in Life and Business* (New York: Random House Canada Limited, 2016).

7   David Usher, *Let the Elephants Run* (Toronto: House of Anansi Press Inc., 2015).

8   Charles Perrow, *Normal Accidents: Living with High Risk Technologies* (Princeton: Princeton University Press, 1986); Samir Shrivastava, Karan Sonpar, Federica Pazzaglia, "Normal Accident Theory versus High Reliability Theory: A resolution and call for an open systems view of accidents," *Human Relations* 62, no. 9 (2009): 1357-1390, https://doi.org/10.1177/0018726709339117.

9   Tim Sullivan, *Embracing Complexity*, Harvard Business Review, https://hbr.org/2011/09/embracing-complexity

10 Brian Tracy, *No excuses!: The Power of Self-Discipline* (New York: Vanguard Press, 2011).

11 Harold McNeill, "A Predictable Accident?," *McNeill Life Stories* (blog), March 22, 2010, https://www.mcneillifestories.com/a-predictable-accident/.

12 Canadian print sales for Self-Help and Personal Growth from 2013 to 2017 increased by 56%, with a 22% increase just between 2016-2017. Accessed January 6, 2019. https://www.booknetcanada.ca/blog/2018/11/13/self-help-personal-growth-book-sales-are-growing

13 Jon C. Jenkins and Maureen R. Jenkins, *The 9 Disciplines of a Facilitator: Leading Groups by Transforming Yourself* (San Francisco: Jossey-Bass, 2006).

14 See for example the IAF Facilitator Core Competencies, item F3. Accessed January 8, 2019. https://www.iaf-world.org/site/professional/core-competencies

15 Howard E. Gardner, *Multiple Intelligences: New Horizons in Theory and Practice* (New York: Basic Books, 2008).

16 Kristen Hansen, http://www.enhansenperformance.com.au/.

17 Matt Church, https://www.mattchurch.com/.

18 Alan Weiss, *Getting Starting in Consulting* (New Jersey: John Wiley & Sons, Inc., 2009).

19 Klaus Manhart, "The Limits of Multitasking," *Scientific American Mind* 14, no. 5 (2004): 62-67, https://www.jstor.org/stable/24997557.

20 Maria Konnikova, "Is Multitasking Everything It's Cut Out To Be? The Brain Says, No," *Big Think*, May 10, 2011, https://bigthink.com/artful-choice/is-multitasking-everything-its-cut-out-to-be-the-brain-says-no.

21 Eyal Ophir, Clifford Nass, and Anthony D. Wagner, "Cognitive control in media multitaskers," *Proceedings of the National Academy of Sciences* 106, no. 37 (2009): 15583-15587, https://doi.org/10.1073/pnas.0903620106.

22 Klaus Manhart, "The Limits of Multitasking," *Scientific American Mind* 14, no. 5 (2004): 62-67, https://www.jstor.org/stable/24997557.

23 Klaus Manhart, "The Limits of Multitasking," *Scientific American Mind* 14, no. 5 (2004): 62-67, https://www.jstor.org/stable/24997557.

24 David F. Swink, "Adrenaline Rushes: Can They Help Us Deal with a Real Crisis?," *Psychology Today*, January 31, 2010, https://www.psychologytoday.com/ca/blog/threat-management/201001/adrenaline-rushes-can-they-help-us-deal-real-crisis; "8 Reasons a Little Adrenaline Can Be a Very Good Thing," *Mental Floss*, http://mentalfloss.com/article/71144/8-reasons-little-adrenaline-can-be-very-good-thing.

25 Chris Hadfield, "What I learned from going blind in space," filmed March 2014 in Vancouver, Canada, TED video, 18:19, https://www.ted.com/talks/chris_hadfield_what_i_learned_from_going_blind_in_space.

26 Stephen M. R. Covey, *The Speed of Trust: The One Thing That Changes Everything* (New York: Free Press, 2008).

27 Chip Heath and Dan Heath, *The Power of Moments: Why Certain Experiences Have Extraordinary Impact* (New York: Simon and Shuster, 2017).

28 Their first illustration is about a "popsicle phone" at The Magic Castle hotel in Beverly Hills. Having stayed there myself, I can attest to how impressed we were with the way an otherwise average hotel incorporated creative details to deliver a memorable stay.

29 Make sure participants have name tags, with their first name printed in a font large enough for you to read from the front of the room. I happen to be excellent at remembering people's names, and it's a little-known facilitation skill that people love. It sets me apart. If that's not your strong point, you need a hack to make it look like you're good at it!

30 Ori Brafman & Rom Brafman, *Click: The Magic of Instant Connections* (New York: Crown Publishing, 2010).

31 Stephen M. Covey, *The 7 Habits of Highly Effective People: Powerful Lessons in Personal Change* (New York: Simon & Schuster, 2013): 188.

32 Warren Berger, *A More Beautiful Question: The Power of Inquiry to Spark Breakthrough Ideas* (New York: Bloomsbury, 2014).

33   Amy Edmondson, *The Fearless Organization: Creating Psychological Safety in the Workplace for Learning, Innovation, and Growth* (New York: John Wiley & Sons Inc., 2018).

34   John Izzo, Jeff Vanderwielen, *The Purpose Revolution: How Leaders Create Engagement and Competitive Advantage in an Age of Social Good* (Oakland: Berrett-Koehler Publishers, Inc., 2018).

35   Thank you to the Institute of Cultural Affairs' (ICA) and Technology of Participation (ToP) for first introducing me to these rational/experiential aims more than 25 years ago. From Wayne and Jo Nelson, *Getting to the Bottom of ToP*, (Bloomington: iUniverse, 2017): 20.

36   David H. Maister, Charles H. Green and Robert M. Galford, *The Trusted Advisor* (New York: Free Press, 2001).

37   John Izzo, Jeff Vanderwielen, *The Purpose Revolution: How Leaders Create Engagement and Competitive Advantage in an Age of Social Good* (Oakland: Berrett-Koehler Publishers, Inc., 2018).

38   Rebecca Sutherns online toolkit: www.rebeccasutherns.com

39   Scott Doorley and Scott Witthoft, Making Space: How to Set the Stage for Creative Collaboration (Hoboken: John Wiley & Sons, 2012).

40   Some examples include:
     Richard M. Ryan and Edward L. Deci, "Self-determination theory and the facilitation of intrinsic motivation, social development, and well-being" *American Psychologist* 55, no. 1 (2000): 68-78, http://dx.doi.org/10.1037/0003-066X.55.1.68.
     Shalini Khazanchi, Therese A. Sprinkle, Suzanne S. Masterson and Nathan Tong, "A Spatial Model of Work Relationships: The Relationship-Building and Relationship-Straining Effects of Workspace Design," Academy of Management Review 43, no. 4 (2018), https://doi.org/10.5465/amr.2016.0240.
     Michael D. Baer, Lisa van der Werff, Jason A. Colquitt, Jessica B. Rodell, Kate P. Zipay and Finian Buckley, "Trusting the "Look and Feel": Situational Normality, Situational Aesthetics, and the Perceived Trustworthiness of Organizations," Academy of Management Journal 61, no. 5 (2018), https://doi.org/10.5465/amj.2016.0248.

41   Provided in the online toolkit at: https://sage-solutions.org/training/free-resource-library/

42   Dana L. Alden, Ashesh Mukherjee & Wayne D. Hoyer, "The Effects of Incongruity, Surprise and Positive Moderators on Perceived Humor in Television Advertising," *Journal of Advertising* 29, no. 2 (2000): 1-15, https://doi.org/10.1080/00913367.2000.106 73605; Allan Filipowicz, "From Positive Affect to Creativity: The Surprising Role of Surprise," *Creativity Research Journal* 18, no. 2 (2006): 141-152, https://doi.org/10.1207/ s15326934crj1802_2.

43   Chris Grams, "The 12 Enemies of Adaptability," *MIX Hackathon*, May 28, 2013, http:// www.mixhackathon.org/hackathon/contribution/12-enemies-organizational-adaptability.

44   See for example: Ingrid Bens. *Facilitating with Ease!: Core Skills for Facilitators, Team Leaders and Members, Managers, Consultants and Trainers* (New Jersey: John Wiley & Sons, Inc., 2018).
     Dorothy Strachan, Paul Tomlinson. *Process Design: Making it Work: A Practical Guide to What to do When and How for Facilitators, Consultants, Managers and Coaches* (San Francisco: Jossey-Bass, 2008).
     Roger M. Schwarz. *The Skilled Facilitator: A Comprehensive Resource for Consultants, Facilitators, Coaches and Trainers* (New Jersey: John Wiley & Sons, Inc., 2017).

Michael Wilkinson. *The Secrets of Facilitation: The S.M.A.R.T. Guide to Getting Results with Groups* (San Francisco: Jossey-Bass, 2004).

45 Charles Perrow, *Normal Accidents: Living with High Risk Technologies* (Princeton: Princeton University Press, 1986).

46 Daniel H. Pink, *When: The Scientific Secrets of Perfect Timing* (New York: Riverhead Books, 2018).

47 Kristen Hansen, http://www.enhansenperformance.com.au/.

48 Martha Lenio, "Leading in Innovative Environments" (presentation, 2017 Municipal Innovators Community Conference, Guelph ON, September 27-28, 2017), http://municipalinnovators.ca/mic-conferences/2017-conference/leading-innovative-environments.

49 John H. Rohrer. "Interpersonal Relationships in Isolated Small Groups" In: Bernard E. Flaherty, *Psychophysiological Aspects of Space Flight* (New York: Columbia University Press, 1961).

50 Robert B. Bechtel & Amy Berning. "The Third-Quarter Phenomenon: Do People Experience Discomfort After Stress Has Passed?" In: A.A Harrison, Y.A. Clearwater & C.P. McKay, *From Antarctica to Outer Space* (New York: Springer, 1991) DOI: 10.1007/978-1-4612-3012-0_24.

51 Daniel H. Pink, *When: The Scientific Secrets of Perfect Timing* (New York: Riverhead Books, 2018).

52 Speaking of which, you're about halfway through the book. Time for an exercise break or a cold drink?

53 Jeffrey M. Ellenbogen, "Cognitive benefits of sleep and their loss due to sleep deprivation," *Neurology* 64, no. 7 (2005): E25-E27, http://dx.doi.org/10.1212/01.wnl.0000164850.68115.81.

54 "UK adults continue to be the worst sleepers in international survey," Aviva, July 21, 2017, https://www.aviva.com/newsroom/news-releases/2017/07/uk-uk-adults-continue-to-be-worst-sleepers-in-international-survey-nearly-20-million-uk-adults1-are-not-getting-the-right-amount-of-sleep-17797/.

55 Rachel Colley, "Ten years of measuring physical activity—What have we learned?," *Statistics Canada*, November 24, 2017, https://www.statcan.gc.ca/eng/blog/cs/physical_activity.

56 I am grateful to Michael Wilkinson of Leadership Strategies for making this intuitive concept explicit for me and for modelling it so well.

57 James Hardy, "Speaking clearly: A critical review of the self-talk literature," *Psychology of Sport and Exercise* 7, no. 1 (2006): 81-97, https://doi.org/10.1016/j.psychsport.2005.04.002.

58 Brené Brown, *Daring Greatly: How the Courage to Be Vulnerable Transforms the Way We Live, Love, Parent and Lead* (New York: Avery, 2012).

59 Donald A. Schon, *The Reflective Practitioner: How Professionals Think in Action* (New York: Basic Books, 1983).

60 Jane Anderson, https://janeandersonspeaks.com.

61 Brian Tracy, Master Your Time, *Master Your Life* (New York: Penguin Random House, 2016).
Maura Nevel Thomas, *Personal Productivity Secrets* (Indianapolis: John Wiley & Sons, 2012).

Peter Bregman, *18 Minutes: Find Your Focus, Master Distraction, and Get the Right Things Done* (New York: Hachette Book Group, 2012).

62 Cal Newport, *Deep Work: Rules for Focused Success in a Distracted World* (New York: Grand Central Publishing, 2016).

63 Lucius Annaeus Seneca

64 Ed Batista, "To Stay Focused, Manage Your Emotions," *Harvard Business Review*, February 2, 2015, https://hbr.org/2015/02/to-stay-focused-manage-your-emotions.

65 Amy Cuddy, *Presence: Bringing Your Boldest Self to Your Biggest Challenges* (Boston: Little, Brown and Company, 2015): 61.

66 Amy Cuddy, *Presence: Bringing Your Boldest Self to Your Biggest Challenges* (Boston: Little, Brown and Company, 2015).

67 Brad J. Schoenfeld, "Attentional Focus for Maximizing Muscle Development: The Mind-Muscle Connection," *Strength and Conditioning Journal* 38, no. 1 (2016): 27-29, https://doi.org/10.1519/SSC.0000000000000190.

68 Chris Grams, "The 12 Enemies of Adaptability," *MIX Hackathon*, May 28, 2013, http://www.mixhackathon.org/hackathon/contribution/12-enemies-organizational-adaptability.

69 See for example:
Susanne Vogel, Lisa Marieke Kluen, Guillén Fernández, Lars Schwabe, "Stress affects the neural ensemble for integrating new information and prior knowledge," *NeuroImage* 173 (2018): 176-187, https://doi.org/10.1016/j.neuroimage.2018.02.038.
Amy Edmondson, *The Fearless Organization: Creating Psychological Safety in the Workplace for Learning, Innovation, and Growth* (New York: John Wiley & Sons Inc., 2018).

70 Kate Bishop, Community Engagement Manager, City of Guelph.

71 Michael Wilkinson, "Identifying Dysfunction – The First Step," *Leadership Strategies*. https://www.leadstrat.com/articles/identifying-dysfunction-the-first-step/.

72 Rebecca Sutherns - https://sage-solutions.org/training/free-resource-library/

73 Amy Edmondson, *The Fearless Organization: Creating Psychological Safety in the Workplace for Learning, Innovation, and Growth* (New York: John Wiley & Sons Inc., 2018): 169.

74 Howard E. Gardener, *Multiple Intelligences: New Horizons in Theory and Practice* (New York: Basic Books, 2008).

75 Chris Hadfield's TED talk illustrates this beautifully. In Canada, the fear of spiders is most definitely higher than the actual danger of them. Belligerent people in meetings are a bit like that.
Chris Hadfield, "What I learned from going blind in space," filmed March 2014 in Vancouver, Canada, TED video, 18:19, https://www.ted.com/talks/chris_hadfield_what_i_learned_from_going_blind_in_space.

76 Sincere thanks to Rick Willis for this insight and many others throughout the book, based on his extensive experience as a facilitator, coach and leader.

77 Ed Catmull, *Creativity, Inc.: Overcoming the Unseen Forces That Stand in the Way of True Inspiration* (Toronto: Random House of Canada, 2014).
Amy Edmondson, *The Fearless Organization: Creating Psychological Safety in the Workplace for Learning, Innovation, and Growth* (New York: John Wiley & Sons Inc., 2018): 174.

78 Nancy Watt, http://nancywattcomm.com/.

79 Brené Brown, *Dare to Lead: Brave Work. Tough Conversations. Whole Hearts* (New York: Random House, 2018).

80 Ibid, p. 261.

81 Note that as per the IAF Code of Ethics, "Our clients include the groups we facilitate [and those who contract with us on their behalf.]" https://www.iaf-world.org/site/professional/iaf-code-of-ethics

82 John Maxwell, *Failing Forward: Turning Mistakes Into Stepping Stones for Success* (Nashville: Thomas Nelson Inc., 2000).

83 Amy Edmondson, *The Fearless Organization: Creating Psychological Safety in the Workplace for Learning, Innovation, and Growth* (New York: John Wiley & Sons Inc., 2018): 160.

84 Ellen Langer, "Learning to Learn from Experience," *Ellen Langer* (blog), http://www.ellenlanger.com/blog/ 121/learning-to-learn-from-experience.

85 Donald A. Schon, *The Reflective Practitioner: How Professionals Think in Action* (New York: Basic Books, 1983).

86 Donald A. Schon, "The Reflective Practitioner," *Oregon State University*, http://oregonstate.edu/instruct/pte/module2/rp.htm.

87 Priya Parker, *The Art of Gathering: How We Meet and Why It Matters* (New York: Penguin Random House LLC, 2018).

88 Yuval Noah Harari, 21 Lessons for the 21st Century (Toronto: McClelland and Stewart, 2018): 269.

89 Amy Edmondson, *The Fearless Organization: Creating Psychological Safety in the Workplace for Learning, Innovation, and Growth* (New York: John Wiley & Sons Inc., 2018): 174.

90 Fia Fasbinder, "Why Every Great Presentation Begins With the End." Accessed January 17, 2019. https://www.inc.com/fia-fasbinder/want-to-give-a-great-speech-take-your-audience-on-.html

Experience Nimble

I have been working with mission-driven leaders around the world for more than 20 years, helping them achieve strategic clarity, spend their time well, and make wiser decisions faster.

I run programs that are nimbly facilitated, and I can teach you and your team to do the same. Do get in touch if you are interested in discussing:

- Keynote speaking

- Facilitation mentoring

- Collaborative strategic planning

In the meantime, follow my blog, "Wiser Decisions Faster" at www.rebeccasutherns.com

With thanks for taking the time to invest in your work and mine,

Rebecca

+1 519 994 0064

rebecca@rebeccasutherns.com

LinkedIn: rebeccasutherns

Twitter: RebeccaSutherns

www.ingramcontent.com/pod-product-compliance
Lightning Source LLC
Chambersburg PA
CBHW071428210326
41597CB00020B/3697